When Your Superpower becomes your Kryptonite

A map to help us find the treasure in ourselves

Tracey Hewitt

When Your Superpower Becomes Your Kryptonite
A map to help us find the treasure in ourselves.

©2015 Tracey Hewitt

Published by Tracey Hewitt
Printed by Ingram Spark, Melbourne Australia

All rights reserved. No part of this publication may be reproduced, distributed, or transmitted in any form or by any means, including photocopying, recording, or other electronic or mechanical methods, without the prior written permission of the publisher, except in the case of brief quotations embodied in critical reviews and certain other non-commercial uses permitted by copyright law.

Disclaimer
All the information, techniques, skills and concepts contained within this publication are of the nature of general comment only and are not in any way recommended as individual advice.
This publication is not intended as a substitute for the advice of health care professionals.

Quotes are attributed within the book

First edition 2015

Editing: nh publishing
Portrait of the author: Caitlyn Hewitt
Cover design, interior design: ezy VA
Cover art: Tracey Hewitt

ISBN 9780994454904 (paperback)
ISBN 9780994454911 (e-book)

For my grandad, Kevin, whose example of living connected to Spirit shines for me to this day

All that any of us aspire to do is to achieve a transparency between our soul and our words. But that is the hardest thing to do, but when you achieve it and walk naked, you will have done your job.

Richard Flanagan, on Australian Story, November 2008

Our map to a CALMER self:

C …. We Choose. Our thoughts, our attitudes, our responses and our actions

A …. Attitude. We can choose a positive one

L …. Like ourselves. Love ourselves. Let our inner voice speak to us kindly

M …. We Matter

E …. Explore our inner selves

R …. We are Responsible - for our own happiness, joy, contentment and satisfaction

When we consciously

CHOOSE our thoughts, actions and

ATTITUDES, we can come to

LIKE ourselves. We understand that we

MATTER, and by

EXPLORING our inner selves, we can accept

RESPONSIBILITY for our own happiness, joy and contentment

Contents

Chapter 1...When your superpower becomes your Kryptonite	Page 7
Chapter 2...Hey Dreamboat! Not you shipwreck.	Page 16
Chapter 3...The perils of pirates and hurricanes	Page 19
Chapter 4...The All or Nothing Song	Page 21
Chapter 5...Managing Muriel	Page 25
Chapter 6...Muriel's friend Fear	Page 34
Chapter 7...Say no to perfection	Page 41
Chapter 8...Compass, maps and harpoon	Page 46
Chapter 9...Chart your course	Page 48
Chapter 10...Savouring every moment	Page 55
Chapter 11...Quit being so damned busy	Page 61
Chapter 12...Do the Downward Facing Dog	Page 67
Chapter 13...Channel your inner Picasso	Page 73
Chapter 14...Find your soulful self	Page 81

Chapter 15...Pen your thoughts						**Page 86**

Chapter 16...Be who you want to be					**Page 93**

Chapter 17...Riding the boundary					**Page 98**

Chapter 18...You've got a radio on board				**Page 104**

Chapter 19...The choice is yours					**Page 107**

Chapter 20...The warm, safe glow of the lighthouse		**Page 113**

Chapter 21...Coming home...to ourselves				**Page 116**

Acknowledgements							**Page 119**

Resources									**Page 120**

Connect with the Author						**Page 121**

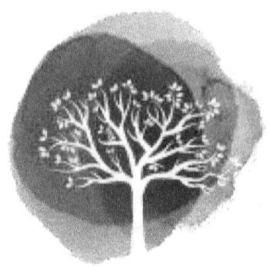

Chapter 1

When your superpower becomes your Kryptonite

And if I asked you to name all the things that you love, how long would it take for you to name yourself? ~Unknown

The monitor beeps urgently, waking me up. Again. After more medical attention than I really want, it becomes clear that the pressing pain in my chest isn't a heart attack. In fact, my heart is in great shape. As I think about it, that's how I ended up in this mess in the first place – a good heart.

Many years earlier, our beloved Dr Bruce explained it to me this way:

"What's happening here with you is something like this: You have a tomato stand, you have loads of tomatoes, and you give your tomatoes away to anyone who would enjoy them. And they're beautiful tomatoes! Everyone loves them, and you love giving them away and seeing how happy they make people, and you're humming along, giving away tomatoes all day because it's so good and everyone loves them, and then one day; you turn around to grab more tomatoes, and there's none left! You've given them all away, and haven't grown more. Your tomato stand is empty."
This resonates with me and makes so much sense that I know what I have to do. I have to take care of myself. Dr Bruce called it anxiety. It's taken a long time, but I now see it for what it is: My superpower

has become my Kryptonite. And that's one wretchedly slippery slope.

I think of a superpower as the thing you do easily, that comes to you effortlessly, that feels great when you're doing it; the thing for which others admire and appreciate you. I recognise that I do possess a small amount of creative Superpower (mostly because the people around me continue to tell me this is so; God bless them!) Caring for others, however, seems to have been my double-edged sword. It is my default setting, my way to negotiate the world, my 'feel good'. And it does feel good! Of course, when a little of something feels good, then a lot of it must be better, right? Fifty years in and I finally understand that is not quite true (Okay, so I'm a slow learner). Because there is a tipping point; a moment in time when the load you have chosen to shoulder to make life happier/better/easier for others becomes too great for you to carry. A moment when your mind, body and spirit baulk, plop down in the corner, bottom lip pouting and say "I don't want to. I can't. I haven't got what it takes. My Dig Deep button is busted."

All the while, I know that I said yes to all of this, that I chose it. But suddenly, what started out as 'feel good' has become overwhelming, draining and simply too much.

I have found myself plopped down in this corner so many times that it makes me question whether I am in fact somehow developmentally delayed. Exactly how many times will I need to end up here before I finally fine tune my navigation system and calibrate it so that I see this corner coming up, and trim my sails rather than smashing headlong into it?

I guess there is an assortment of habits or character traits (some may even call them flaws...) that contribute to my superpower turning on me. I expect a lot of myself. There, I said it. I admitted it. I am the gentlest friend and supporter and am constantly telling others that they need to be kind to themselves and I deeply believe it's a basic act we all need to engage in - self-compassion. It's high time I learned that song by heart.

One instance in particular stands out as the ultimate example of choosing my own undoing:

My son Keelan and his fiancee Madi were looking forward to their engagement party at our home. The date has been set and a few ideas tossed around about the format of this celebration which would also honour Madi turning 21. A week or two before the invitations are to go out and they have a very big announcement. They're expecting a baby! Now this isn't exactly the way they had it planned in their minds but after the initial surprise, they are delighted, and we are happy to be adding to our quickly growing clutch of grandbabies. I drift off to sleep that night getting my head around the notion of my baby being a father and feeling just a little twinge of sadness in the middle of the joy. Will they ever get the wedding they have been planning and looking forward to? Perhaps they will, but will they enjoy it the same way with a little one as part of the package? (I expect there are many mums out there who have had this discussion with themselves at two in the morning).

The next evening - a Friday night - they come to visit us once again, with a big question. "Since we already have the engagement party planned and everyone will be here anyway, what do you think about us surprising everyone by getting married at the party?"

I am all in. This feels like a great idea - fun, happy, exciting...all the good stuff. In a couple of hours, we had formulated the bones of a plan and knew what needed to happen. A surprise wedding - yes! Let's do this! With astonishing speed and serendipity, the important details fell into place. By the end of that weekend, Madi had a dress, Keelan had chosen suits, and they had wedding bands, a celebrant and caterers. In nine weeks, they would be saying 'I do' in our garden, in the backyard Keelan had grown up in.

We discovered that they had quietly always wanted this to be the place where they tied the knot but after us having many conversations where we said that you'd have to be mad to have a wedding in your own backyard, neither of them thought they could even suggest it. Now I've never uttered this to another soul, but I had always had a little daydream about the boys getting married here too. That is where my practical side always pulled me up. We live in the middle of a paddock, our nearest town has one pub and limited accommodation, there are no taxis, we have a low level river crossing that floods easily, and our alternate access is very much 4WD only. Caterers would have to come from 200km away. Now there are lots of sensible, practical and logical reasons why a wedding in our garden is a crappy idea. Yet we were all set to have 120 guests to an engagement party/21st; so why not toss in a wedding ceremony too?

The sense of excitement and fun lasted only for a short while. Then the reality of keeping this a secret got its claws into me. There was a wedding and another grandbaby on the way; two secrets to keep to myself. In the course of the next nine weeks, I ended up clutching so many secrets belonging to other people to my chest that I was barely able to speak to anyone for fear of letting something slip.

A couple of weeks before the wedding, I was trying desperately to concentrate on paying some bills when my head went white. As in, the inside of my head felt cold and I lost the room around me for a moment. The strangest feeling washed over me, and I knew that all I could do in that moment was crawl onto the floor and lie there until the sensation passed. This experience scared the hell out of me. The calm, rational voice in my head that I've come to trust as my 'knowing' says to 'just stay calm, this is stress, lots of stress, which you need to manage - NOW'. I laid there for a while breathing deeply trying to focus on anything I'd learned in yoga class to help centre and calm myself. I'm not sure how long I was there but I eventually opened my eyes, sat up, and got back to what I was doing, telling myself I would do more in the future to stay calm. I would do that after I finished paying the bills, weeding six garden beds, putting the ironing away, letting the caterer know about numbers, rewriting that list of little jobs that needed to be done in the next two weeks, cleaning the spare room, making sure the lawn was being watered evenly and arranging collection of the portable cold room and tables and chairs. I also needed to check on my young friend whom I was desperately concerned might harm herself and I was obsessively worried about my daughter-in-law Leah and her body doing battle with her autoimmune disorder ITP and being pregnant all at once. I needed to set an alarm to remind me to go outside at 3pm to observe the best spot to set up tables for the wedding ceremony, and…what was I promising I'd do again? Oh yes, do more to care for myself. Yes, I'll definitely do that after the wedding.

But nine weeks is just too long to put yourself aside - especially when there is a degree of stress in your life. Looking back on that time, I can clearly see what I allowed to happen. I chose to be busy. I chose anxiety. I chose to push and strive and expect myself to accomplish too much, while at the same time being completely available to anyone who wanted me for anything. But, and most dangerously, I chose to act as though I was just fine with all of this. I chose to pretend to everyone - even myself, especially myself - that I could handle all of this. I felt that I was calm and in control; that nothing fazed me. But I was kidding myself. And I possibly fooled a few of the people around me as well.

The irony of the whole situation is that if I had chosen to spend half an hour every morning practicing yoga and meditating, devoted a little time to writing my journal or taking an ambling walk in the fresh air, I would indeed have been able to handle it all. But I decided to set down all the tools I knew I could rely on, telling myself there simply wasn't time right now and I could pick them up again later. I have very few regrets in this life. However that decision is possibly my biggest.

Yet the experience has led me to examine my life and my choices and ultimately to a much healthier, contented, wiser place. So perhaps it's time I let go of the regret and grab the lesson tightly and grow it into something wonderful.

One baby step at a time, I began unearthing my own wisdom. Slowly, as I tried a kinesiology session here, a long yoga session there and lots of painting and journaling, an old idea floated to the surface. I wanted to write a book. This time, instead of making some half-baked attempt and letting the other various commitments in my life sweep it aside, I made what would prove to be a monumental decision. I contacted a coach. Kerrie set up camp on my sideline, and started cheering. Gradually, with her coaxing and reassurance, I excavated the bones of this book.

I thought I was going to write a book about my life as a city girl turned farmer's wife. It would be illustrated with my artwork and encouraging my readers to try art journaling.
Then one morning, I woke from a vivid dream. I did my best to capture the details of it in my journal:

I am carrying a bag, it looks like a bowling ball bag. It is light-colored, made of leather and has little stubby, short handle. There is a bright light glowing inside it, spilling out through the tiny splits in the opening at the top. The light is all the possible ways I might do this.

I take the bag to my favorite tree. Alone. Safe. It's dark and cool and quiet. I settle myself under the safety of its branches. A gentle breeze rustles the leaves. I sit for a while with this bag beside me, its quiet glow feeling like a promise and a threat all at once. Where did I get this bag from? It's been with me all my life. From my parents, my grandparents. It's been filling up with insights and experience. I guess I've never noticed it before because its light wasn't shining. But now it fairly threatens to blow the bag apart if I don't open it, share it, light up the night with it. It feels scary though. I don't know what will happen when I open it. Will it be overwhelming and dangerous to ME? Will it draw too much attention to me? Can I manage and handle what happens once I open it? Will people that I can't love or don't like come to the light? Will my special people still be close to me, or will they be washed away in a flood? Will absolutely NOTHING happen? Will it be a blinding flash that disappears into the darkness, never to be seen again? I have so many questions, sitting here beside this bag - excited and afraid in equal measure. No, in truth, I am more afraid. What am I scared of? That if I open this bag, everything will change? I don't want to go back to being pulled in a million directions. I'm afraid I may not be able to handle what comes when I open it. I'm afraid that when I open it, it will be nothing. That I've been kidding myself and everyone else all this time. I'm afraid of getting tied down and losing the loose freedom of my days.

And, I'm really scared it might be amazing. What is it that's holding me in, wanting to keep small? It's safe. It's comfortable. I can manage it. What else? There's a bit of "don't get too big for your boots; don't blow your own trumpet; keep quiet, be nice, fit in and belong and stay the same as everyone else or you'll be excluded and left out and criticised..."

It's time. Open the damned bag!

I pull the bag close beside me, and slowly, carefully, pull it open. For a second, the tiniest bit of light shines out. Then, as I fully open it, I am surrounded by beautiful, warm, bright, gorgeous light. There are colours like fireworks, only more beautiful. It swirls around me, pops and sparkles and I feel warm, calm, uplifted, excited, inspired, and buzzing with a deep contented joy. The light and energy gather in my belly, intensify, explode and float around me. The sparks are set in orbit now, rotating like satellites around a sun. Wow.

I then realised that this is more about nourishing me than it is about giving to others. It's about caring for myself.

So, I ask myself, what do you want to do? What will nourish you that can help and support others as a by-product?

What do you long to do?

Write a book. For me. Live, love and care for me...

Write a story for myself.
When I look into the bottom of the bag, there is still light. And there's a book. Fat, square and light-coloured, with illuminated gold-gilded lettering. There are coloured plates among the pages.

It's heavy in my hands.

What I realised from my dream is that it's all about seeking and connecting with the best of myself so that I can give my best to others.

When your superpower becomes your Kryptonite is about how to get back up when you have fallen, weakened and deplete, because what makes you great has just knocked you down. It's about how I am discovering that I can use my superpower to help and give love and support to others, without it being at the expense of my own health and wellbeing.

Okay then, sounds simple doesn't it? I had no idea where or how to begin. Kerrie helped by giving me a few questions to answer. As I spent more time cogitating and exploring, the ephemeral nature of this idea began to take a more solid form.

The exploration began with adding an image to where I was situated at the start of this journey, and where I wanted to go in the future. That image began as a seedling just sprouted, its roots already deep down, and new leaves beginning to sprout. The picture of where I wanted to end up was a tree.

A sprawling, old, beautiful evergreen tree with a dense canopy. It sits at the top of a gentle, green slope. It has plank swings and shade and cool resting places. Its trunk is smooth and warm - perfect to sit back against - and it radiates calm strength. The tree represents wisdom, knowledge, safety and protection, nurturing, allowing.

Beneath the tree is a group of women - they are sure of themselves, confident, they understand life has ups and downs and to embrace the rough patches as an important part of the journey. It's an opportunity to grow, learn and expand. They believe in themselves and have examined their inner worlds.

They reached the safety of the tree through pain, hurt, doing things they didn't believe they could do, stopping, listening to themselves and starting again. They got there with the help of meditation, movement, journaling, spiritual practice, helping others, practicing gratitude, engaging their creativity, resting and questing. Mostly, they arrived there as a result of their choices.

This tree represents to me our safe piece of terra firma. A place to rest and celebrate after life has had us sailing through the roaring forties and the doldrums, negotiating the reefs and wild weather, and defending our treasure against pirates.

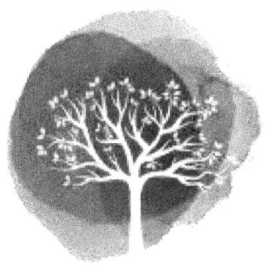

Chapter 2

Hey Dreamboat! Not you shipwreck...
A ship in a harbour is safe, but that is not what ships are built for.
~John A Shedd

Imagine a sleek, shiny, fabulous-looking vessel moored in the harbor, sparkling in the warm sunshine and looking seaworthy and inviting. That's how I think we look when we're fully in superpower mode. Get that baby out on the ocean, into some rough weather, add some poor navigation and throw a boatload of pirates at it.... shipwreck coming up.

I believe we all have a superpower unique to each of us, something which brings us a sense of deep power and contentment when we flex our superpower muscles and bring forth the good it enables.

I first encountered this idea while working through an eCourse with Brene Brown. If you're unfamiliar with Dr Brown and her work on wholeheartedness, shame and vulnerability, I'll wait here for you. Put this book down, go acquaint yourself with her and come back when you're ready.

One of the lessons from that was to identify your superpower and your Kryptonite. She suggests thinking about them as two ends of one continuous line. Your superpower is at the end where there is strength and grace and it feels strong and authentic. The Kryptonite hangs out at the opposite end of the continuum. When taken to extremes or turned upside down to reveal its opposite, your superpower becomes the thing that causes your unravelling.

I've come to see the transition of dreamboat to shipwreck as a good analogy for the journey of our superpower becoming our Kryptonite.

Within our superpower, we sail out of a safe harbor; clean, fresh, ready for anything and loaded with enthusiasm, energy, love and excitement. The sun shines, breeze caresses and freedom reigns. We come across some rough weather; windy, raining and uninspiring and are blown ever so slightly off course. We don't notice though, because the next day is sunny and deliciously clear and crisp, and we leave our bad weather behind us. Of course, we continue to encounter runs of foul weather, each one blowing us a little more off course, and our problems begin to magnify, but we don't really notice. We feel strong, capable and, well, like a superpower nothing can touch.

We continue sailing though the clear beautiful days, and the rainy, windy days, not giving much thought to the direction which we set our sails when we began. When we are left battered and knocked about by a hurricane, it finally occurs to us to check our bearings, and we discover we are not only way off course, but quite likely in the wrong bloody ocean. Which sends us into an anxious panic, because we are expected to deliver this cargo in two weeks and right now, we're so far off course we'll be lucky to make it in two years.

In the dead of night, restless and pushing hard to get back on course, we discover pirates have boarded our dreamboat, and suddenly we are fighting - possibly for our lives. The fight causes structural damage and we begin to take on water.

As we start sinking, we watch, numb, and wonder how we got into this mess. At this point, we have two choices. Sink. Shipwreck. Or we can access all the navigational and support tools within our reach. The good news is that all those tools are on board. We have them within us. The frustrating news is that had we accessed them earlier - about the time of that first bout of bad weather - we may have avoided finding ourselves here. The life-altering news is that if we touch base with these tools every day, course correcting as we go and paying careful attention to our surroundings, we would most likely have made it to our destination, delivered our bounty, and been celebrating with champagne, surrounded by our loved ones by now.

Our dreamboats are equipped with everything we need to navigate every journey. It's up to us though to familiarise ourselves with the tools, learn how to use them best and discover which tools are the most useful, which tools we enjoy using the most and those that deliver the best results. It is up to each individual to captain their own ship and plot their own course, carefully choosing the tools and techniques that best fit the journey.

The journey though this book will take us through that bad weather and close enough to the pirates to identify them for future reference. But the biggest part of this journey is discovering what our navigational tools are and how to use them to make the course corrections we all need to keep us heading towards our chosen destination. Once we have discovered what we need, it then comes down to using them. This is about making a conscious decision about where our power lies. Every minute of every day, we have a choice. And I believe that is our real superpower. Our ability to choose, our attitude, our environment, our expectations, our level of acceptance, our fight and knowing when it's time to graciously stand down.

For if we live as though we have no choice, we become weakened and depleted, laid bare by our Kryptonite.

Work Cited: Oprah's Lifeclass in Brene Brown's e-course - *The Gifts of Imperfection,* oprah.com 2013

Chapter 3

The perils of pirates and hurricanes
*When I try to be everything for everyone else, I lose me.
And that's who they wanted in the first place. ~ Unknown*

There's a reason why pirates want to plunder our dreamboat. It's because we are transporting a tremendous treasure! It makes sense that we should know just what that precious cargo is before we set sail. The knowledge motivates us to learn how to protect it and take care of it in the long-term.

If we don't protect it, our boat is likely to be sunk, and the world will never benefit from our treasure. What good is it if we don't deliver it safe and intact? I think I may have spent an inordinate amount of time trying to figure out what my treasure is. I also suspect that I'm not alone. But what I'm coming to realise is that our treasure is us. Our soul, our essence, our precious selves, exactly as we are, authentic, real and raw. That's what the world wants from us. It's the only truly unique gift we can offer.

If we were to walk through our day today, thinking of ourselves as treasures, how might it influence the choices we make? The words we speak to ourselves? What we eat? When we rest? What might we choose to do to safeguard our treasure, instead of plundering it?

What might our lives begin to look like, how might our days feel, if we regarded ourselves as treasures? Every. Single. Day.

What if we also began to regard others in our lives - even those fleetingly passing through our lives - as treasures? How might it change the way we listen? The way we speak? The things we look for and notice in others? I believe that when we look at ourselves, and others, as treasures, expecting to see value and jaw-dropping beauty, that belief and expectation can shift us to a place of loving acceptance.

When we set off on our journey in our dreamboats, we can't imagine the perils and pitfalls that lie in wait for us as we head towards open waters. Hurricanes and pirates can throw us off track or sink us completely.

I'm sure there are lots of other potential calamities than we'll look at here, but these are the ones I'm most familiar with. The ones that I've learned the hard way will have me taking on water, or being set adrift and lost at sea.

The Inner Critic, Fear and Perfectionism get top billing in this rundown of lurking dangers. Then there's what I call - for want of a better description -

The All or Nothing Song.

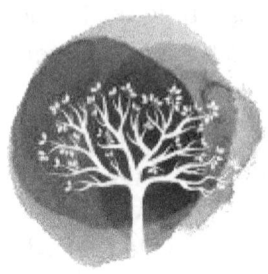

Chapter 4

The All or Nothing Song
Something has to change, and it's me.
~ Petrea King

I'm standing under the shower quietly seething. After 33 years, I'm STILL the only one in the kitchen at 8.30 at night cleaning up the dinner dishes, while his lordship sleeps on the couch. I must have told him a million times how much this pisses me off. No one ever helps me. I'm so sick of being the only one who cares about this house. Just for once, I'd like to be on the top of his list. We never do what I want. It's always all about what he wants...

On and on it goes. Please tell me I'm not the only one who has this garbage rattling around in their heads sometimes. One of the signals that I'm not looking after myself is this exact inner dialogue. The one where I'm on a steep slope of resentment and frustration and it's all everyone else's fault. The one where I tell myself I deserve better - which is ironic, because I do, and I know I do, so why the hell don't I look after myself better?

What? Wait! Hang on, it's everyone else who should be looking after me better. Isn't it?

Well actually, no. I've come to believe I'm not alone in finding myself singing this All or Nothing Song, but here's the thing: when we feel unappreciated, it's usually because we aren't appreciating ourselves. When we feel unloved - you guessed it - it's usually because we don't love ourselves. These days, thoughts or comments that include "you always" or "you never" or "no-one ever" or "everybody" are red flags waving to tell me that whatever my bitch is, it may be more about what I'm not giving myself than it is about what anyone else might not be giving me.

Those "all or never" mutterings are an alarm. When I hear myself pour out the "No-one ever helps me" line, I know it's time to stop. To quietly and compassionately ask myself "Is this true?" Of course it isn't. There are most likely 30 instances of help I've received from others since lunch time yesterday. But have I helped myself? Ah...I guess not.

Funnily enough, I found myself singing this tune just a couple of days ago. In fact, it wasn't funny at all; it was excruciating. Haymaking and harvest time, as any farmer's wife will tell you, brings long, chaotic days. It's a season filled with unpredictable requests for meals at odd times, ferrying people and machinery all over the place and solitary dinners ahead of tucking yourself into bed secure in the knowledge that the phone will ring or the two-way radio will spring to life and jolt you awake at least once in the wee hours. It's hardly the bucolic bliss that a rural existence can offer. In all honesty, it's the absolute pits. The farmer in my life narrows his attention. His focus is laser sharp on the task at hand. This means that any chance of him focusing even a shred of attention on me, or any help or support I might need is about as likely as a snowball's existence in hell. To be fair, he is running on around three hours' sleep in every 24 hours and keeping that up, on and off, for weeks. Haymaking and harvest are among our biggest income earners and the success of these endeavours largely determines our success in staying viable as a business.

Because our usual routine is shot to hell, it's all too easy for me to abandon the small acts that contribute to me staying on course. That 10 minutes of yoga and breathing right after breakfast? Forget it, someone needs a lift to the paddock. Making a few plans to be sure the important stuff gets done? What's the point, someone will need me somewhere else in a hurry, and it won't get done anyway. Make something? Ha! Not in this circus! Before I know it, my commitment to being available and supportive to the success of this operation feels like a weight around my ankle that is pulling me under and I'm resenting everyone and everything. This gets to the point that where I grumble that I'd like a wife, and the man who loves me (even when I'm not at all loveable) says that I'd be missing out, because he already has the best one in the world. Instead of savouring his acknowledgement, I roll my eyes and keep on with the "you never" and "I always" accusations. Of course, it took a lot of journal writing, walking and a long yoga session and meditation to haul myself back to a place where anyone could bear to be near me and where I could stand to live with myself. If I had simply developed my own laser focus and made certain that I slipped in a couple of quick kindnesses and cared for myself enough to be able to give 300 percent to the demands of the season, I would have been okay. And I would not have started singing that stinking All or Nothing Song!

I found this most recent version of the song especially difficult, because these days I know it's a sign that I'm off-course. I know it's the signal to look at myself and make a course correction. The thing about the All or Nothing Song is that it says that everyone else is responsible and that someone else needs to fix it. But, these days, I know the singer is also the repairer.

Now, don't get me wrong. If someone is in a situation where the undeniable truth is that they're being completely unappreciated and disrespected, then no amount of looking within for the root of unhappiness will change those circumstances. But, that person has a choice. They can continue to live with the issue as best they can or choose to remove themselves. We always have a choice. Sometimes, we would give anything for a third or fourth option - an option that won't unravel our lives and send our relationships into turmoil. The important thing to recognise is that there is always a choice. Choosing to do nothing is still a choice. When we recognise that our circumstances and situations are the product of our own choosing, it is only then that we can recover our power.

There are countless ways I can be blown off-course. Sometimes, I'll notice that I'm not where I want to be. A quick course correction will remedy that with ease. But when I start hearing myself chant 'You Never', 'I Always,' 'Everyone Always', 'No-one Ever' and all of their relatives, I know that I need to get up to the bridge and start using those instruments immediately. The alternative is to wallow in the bluesy notes of the All or Nothing Song. Only one of those things frees me to get back to living wholeheartedly with joy and appreciation. You know those songs that get stuck in your head and quickly start to drive you crazy because you can't seem to find a way to make them stop? The All or Nothing Song is one of those. It takes some effort and intention to shift that sucker. Like the Lamb Chop Song, the only really effective way to stop it running on repeat is to put on a different song. Try a song that engages and delights you, in order to banish the annoying tune for a while. To reset your brain, I recommend the Gratitude Song as a wonderful place to start.

Chapter 5

Managing Muriel

*You've been criticising yourself for years, and it hasn't worked.
Try approving of yourself and see what happens*
~Louise Hay

Muriel lives in my head.

She is the voice of what some people would call the inner critic. She only really found her name a year or so ago, but that battle-axe has had a voice forever. Such a nasty voice, too. I am led to believe we all have this voice, and sometimes, it has some truly useful advice for us.

"You won't make it across two lanes of traffic before that truck – wait!"

"If you open that second bottle of wine, you'll regret it in the morning."

At times, Muriel undoubtedly keeps me safe. Or at least keeps me from regretful hangovers. For this protection, I am deeply thankful and appreciative. So, she gets to stay. However, that old broad can get going on some mean, nasty monologues.

The arrival of menopause brought with it the expected hot flushes, strange moods and inexplicable anxiety. It also turned that voice in my head into a hateful, middle-aged version of the cast of Mean Girls.

"You are so-o fat."

"You can't wear that, you look stupid."

"Don't even try to do that – you suck at it anyway."

"You're getting old…getting old… getting old…"

You get the idea. Fat, old, ugly and awful. Useless and past your use by date. Where was this coming from? She'd been tough on me for years, but she was upping the ante and if I kept listening for one more minute, life was going to become one long parade of granny knickers, sensible shoes and giving up on my dreams.

Enter the Inner Critic Intervention. Without having any idea what I was doing, I started writing in my journal:

What the hell am I doing? I want to be a vibrant, excited, energised, cool, amazing, fun, lively person who smashes life and all it has to offer. And yet here I sit like a bloody couch potato with nothing - zilch, zip, nada, zero, nothin'. One day slides into the next with little achieved and a bit more self-flagellation for good measure. I want to start this art journalling group. My hands and feet are super-neglected. As are my eyebrows and hair. I need to lose – I don't know – maybe 5 or 10 kilos. Maybe that book I want to write is about art journalling. Art journalling as therapy.

"Oh good – that's working out for you, isn't it?"

Shut UP, Muriel! I think it's time I bloody well evicted her.

Okay Muriel, old girl – tell me what you think. I do know that listening to you is sometimes very helpful. Here is your open invitation to tell me what I'm doing wrong, how I'm failing. You have three minutes. Dust the flour off your apron, straighten up those cat's eye glasses and go:

"Well! It's about time you actually listened to me! You are so damned lazy! Get off your butt, stop swanning around 'feeling' and 'thinking' and 'cogitating', just do something. Actually just do it. I don't know why you can't do it all. You just need a routine, and some commitment. You're the biggest flake ever. All those people in your life who interrupt you – well, you just have to tell them you're not available every minute of every damn day. You need to have that house clean, the baking tins full, that yard tidy and beautiful. THEN you can tackle that office and get things in order and after you've taken care of all that, you can go off and play in that studio. You do know that's just silly, don't you? It's not serious work you carry on with in there – it's not even important! You need to be organised, prepared and perfect. And you shouldn't need all that 'looking after yourself' time. You don't deserve that luxury. Only self-indulgent, spoilt rich bitches get that. You have to work. Work hard. Struggle, even. Then you might deserve something. Get up off that couch. Stop writing your complaints – for heaven's sake, if you did what needed doing instead of writing about how hard it is, you'd have it all done!"

Thanks Muriel. I fucking hate you. But, right now I'm having trouble seeing you as separate from me. And, I'm buying and believing all of that. What about this seed of an idea that Art Journalling as Therapy could be a book?

"Well, since you hardly even do any, that's not much of a start. And look at you! You're hardly a shining example of mental health and the benefits of an artful existence, are you? If you got off your ever- expanding arse and did something, maybe."

Okay Muriel. I thank you for your thoughts and acknowledge that I need to set some boundaries and need to find some passion. Is there a way you could help me with those things? I know you do have some wisdom, and I'd love your support. I really find your negative chatter debilitating though. Could we do a deal that I'll try really hard to move forward and accomplish things if you promise to speak positively to me instead of criticising me? I'd really like that – because I do believe you are trying to tell me things I need to know, but I can't hear them above the negative criticisms, which just hurt and shut me down.

Okay, I'll try. How about you start by exploring the idea a bit? Do some journal pages about this shit you're in journey you're on. Use me as a place to start. Quieting the inner critic. Draw me – don't forget my apron and cat's eye glasses! And see what develops. Photograph the process. Write a blog post or two. Submit to a magazine or two. Start teaching art journalling classes. What is stopping you?

It was at this point that I burst out laughing because I realised that Muriel (whom I had named only 10 minutes earlier) could be my Grade 9 high school Home Economics teacher, Miss Anderson. This woman had a terribly unfortunate voice, and was possibly the most negative human being I had encountered in my 14 or so years up to that point. She would habitually hawk up some spit onto her fingers to wipe chalk off the blackboard. Unfortunately, she would also swipe her finger through one cake batter after another in the Home Economics kitchen, suck it off, and move on to the next bowl until she had tasted them all, never once washing that finger off. And yes, she probably had spat on it to clean the blackboard first. Toss in sarcastic and a tiny bit mean, and sadly, somewhat dowdy and dull. Not that I consider this a character flaw but it affected my opinion of her back then. She was always clad in sensible dresses, sensible shoes, and we (in the way of most teenage girls) believed her to be almost terminally uncool. We were certain that she never had any fun. EVER. Even now, I can hear her shrill voice and see the spittle *flying across the room as she bobbed up from looking into one of the ovens. "Whose jam tarts are these?" she screeched.*

They were mine.
The only problem was on that particular day we were cooking jam drops. Whoops...

Having given Muriel not only a name, but a whole persona, suddenly I was able to do something with her. An art journal page came together fast. A brush and ink sketch (she ended up looking much younger and more attractive than I remembered of my former teacher), a quickly-written unflattering description, and the announcement that 'Muriel needs a makeover' was born. More writing was added to the facing page, and in no time, I had put that dragon in her place once and for all.

Guess what Muriel? I'm not listening! And...hold onto your control briefs...I just gave you sparkly turquoise glasses, hot pink lips and burnt that ugly dress!

From now on, here's how it goes: you're in my head so you're on MY side, dammit! When you have something useful to tell me (and I know sometimes you do) how about you offer it nicely? No more negative, squally, mean comments. If you see a better way, go ahead and offer it – kindly.

Muriel, what I need from you is love, protection and wisdom.
I think you totally rock those turquoise glasses, by the way.
Let's start over, shall we?

And start over we did. Of course, sometimes she forgets herself, and gets going with the nasty stuff again, but these days – mostly – I call her on it.

"Muriel!"

I say it in the same tone in which you'd scold your dog just as it lifts its leg to pee on your mother-in-law's handbag. Except when it comes to Muriel, I tell her to 'shut the hell up!'

Writing and drawing are immensely helpful vehicles to take us on a journey and hopefully, illuminate things which perhaps are unclear to us in spite of endless hours of thinking and worrying and turning thoughts over and over.

I did put together those art journalling classes. Not only did I put them together, but people signed up, showed up and asked for more! Somewhere along the way, I realised something. As I already mentioned, I suck at self- compassion. Or at least, up until recently I have. During the course of delivering these art journalling workshops to an ever-growing group of beautiful women, I discovered I was not alone in all of this. In fact, I'm almost beginning to think the world is experiencing a lack of self-compassion crisis! Here's the thing: if we don't treat ourselves kindly, how can we expect others to? Oh sure, there's the old tune which goes something like this: "I give out what I want to get back and treat others the way I want to be treated so why do I feel so used?" Believe me, I know that song too! I've sung it myself for years. And I believe that in essence, the first part is true. Put out what you want to get back, good karma and all that. BUT - and this is a big but - we have to treat ourselves every bit as kindly and thoughtfully as we treat others, we must be our own best friends. It starts with me treating myself in the way I want others to be treated. Treating myself with the consideration and respect I would extend to any other human being.

When I dug out the journal page I've shared here about my conversation with my inner critic, I cringed. I felt physically ill.

"What kind of woman speaks to her own precious self like that?" I wondered. I've had this venomous, cruel narrative running on repeat for years. It's a wonder I hadn't gone stark raving, bat shit crazy! After I sat with the shame of having literally abused myself (I realised in that moment I had done this for as long as I could remember), I began to notice something else. There was another voice there. A voice that was compassionate and kind, gentle and forgiving in spite of the appalling cruelty of the other. A voice that could continue to be respectful. Okay, so it did tell Muriel to eff off, but hey, I figure some strong language was required to make that old bitch sit up and pay attention! I may have perhaps questioned whether I was in fact schizophrenic, but I looked around and figured that no-one else seemed to think I was nuts, and this felt healthy, really...

This other voice, I finally realised, is my self-compassion. My inner wise woman, if you will. The best version of me. Hell, I really saw this chick as a bloody Rock Star. That's the way to shut down that old dragon!

So I made a choice. I chose to speak to myself the way I would speak to my best friend. I've always academically understood that the idea of being our own best friend is the only way to really have any other relationships. We've all heard over and over that others can't love us until we love ourselves. I seem to have taken a long time to move from understanding it on a purely academic level to actually 'getting it' with my gut. I decided I would never let myself speak in any way that I wouldn't allow with my most precious friends. Try it - it's amazing. You have to stop a lot mid-thought, take a deep breath and ask yourself: What would I say to Deb if she had just driven the 40km round trip to town and back, only to arrive home without the Tick Fever Vaccine the men needed for that mob of new bulls that just trucked in this morning? Would I call her a friggin' idiot? Would I tell her she's a complete waste of space? Of course not! In fact I can't imagine under what circumstances I would ever be moved to say that to a friend. So why the hell would I speak to myself that way then? Self-compassion, it seems to me, is the most challenging gift we are called upon to give ourselves. The words we whisper to ourselves are ones that only we can hear, the gentleness we extend to our broken places, to our pain, our hurt and our fear is ours alone.

Being kind to yourself takes practice and lots of it. The moment I seriously decided I was writing this book and set myself a deadline, Muriel lost her shit. My chest was tight, my mind was spinning and Muriel was freaking out. It was as though she was pacing in furious circles in my head, every now and again stopping to shriek "Stay small!"

Sorry Muriel, not this time. I've got your number these days, and just as soon as you're ready, we'll sit down and you can tell me what it is you're scared of, and we'll face that and get on with this. Giving that inner critic part of myself a separate identity helps to separate and isolate the fear and negative self-talk. It's easier to have a conversation, easier to reassure myself. At the bottom of it all, that is what I need. Muriel is simply trying to keep me safe and protect me. But she's a fearful old broad and the only way to quiet her down is for self-compassion to step up, kindly and gently listen to Muriel, acknowledge her fears, thank her for showing me where I need to pay attention and check for booby traps or monsters under the bed. She needs to be reassured, to be promised that I'm keeping safe and firmly told that fear isn't winning this time.

I suspect there could be a thousand reasons why any of us might not find it easy to speak kindly to ourselves. Some people spend their lives holding their parents responsible for their wounds and shortcomings, others blame teachers, school bullies, griefs, accidents or illnesses. But do you know what? Ruminating over the causes and blaming other people or events for the harsh way we treat ourselves only serves to keep us caught up in our own misery. I've spent some wasted hours contemplating where exactly this might have come from, this need I seem to have within me to be perfect in order to be of value. Who knows? And really, who cares? I can decide, as of right now, that I am in fact, worthy of being loved and accepted for who I am, the way I am - faults, shortcomings, extra kilos, mouldy shower recess, and all.

Chapter 6

Muriel's friend Fear

The cave you fear to enter holds the treasure you seek
~ Joseph Campbell

Fear is Muriel's best friend. In fact, I think Fear is where Muriel gets the fuel for her flaming Molotov Cocktail thoughts of negativity, the ones she throws into my head right when I'm sailing along well. They are designed to blow me right off course and question whether I am capable of making the journey at all.

Fear has many faces. There's terror, which is the kind of fear I felt one ordinary Sunday evening as I was handing out ice cream cones for dessert to our three boys, their visiting friends (the local constable's two little daughters) and my nephew. The children in our care that night ranged from nine years old down to three and there were six kids in total. They were all at our house for a super-sized sleepover when my husband Alan answered a call.

He dropped the phone, grabbed a shotgun and yelled: "Get the kids on the floor, someone's attacked Dad." He took off outside, fired a couple of shots into the darkness at the front of the house which overlooked an empty paddock. Then, gun in hand, he quickly made his way around the outside of our home, locking doors as he went.

As my Nanna indicated when she used to tell people "Tracey lives in the middle of a paddock", we live in the middle of nowhere, miles from anywhere and anyone. At that time, Alan's parents lived in one of the only other two houses on the 10,000 acre property, 80 yards from our place. The lovely big windows were bare as curtains were a long way down the list of priorities in our new house, which we'd moved into just months earlier. So there we were, huddled on the floor, using the lounge chairs as our only flimsy form of protection, ice cream now dripping from their tiny elbows. Nothing ruins your appetite like an armed intruder.

We didn't ever see the masked man. My father-in-law Gunny had phoned telling us to lock the doors. He'd been hurt - his knee was busted while his wife Loye had been badly cut. We pieced together over the next couple of hours that Loye had heard a crash outside. Thinking that a cat had knocked over a pot plant, she went to clean it up, only to be met at the back door by a tall man wearing a balaclava and waving a gun at her, demanding that she get back inside. Gunny was convinced the intruder was going to kill them both in their own home, but he wasn't having that! They wrestled briefly, but Gunny soon found himself grounded and on the receiving end of the unwanted guest's boots, with the tread marks lasting on the side of his face for days. Loye launched herself at the intruder from the top step, knocking the gun out of his hand. Next thing she knew, he had pulled a knife out, cutting her hand badly as he waved it around. When she started bleeding, he quickly fled, leaving them both stunned and battered. All we knew of our unwelcome visitor was that he had arrived fully armed and looking for something. Whatever it was, he didn't get it. And, as far as we knew, he was outside somewhere with a gun and a knife while we were commando crawling around on the floor, utterly unable to answer the girls' fearful question: "Is our Daddy going to get shot?" I wasn't sure we weren't all going to be front page news before breakfast.

Thankfully, the police arrived and eventually a detective took the girls home to their mum. Fortunately, their dad didn't get shot, and neither did anyone else.

There was a close call though for Theo, the dog belonging to the couple working for us at the time. The police had set up camp in Loye and Gunny's house for the night in case the intruder returned, and Theo's arrival a few hours later caused our dog to start barking frantically which brought the police running, guns at the ready... This set off a great commotion in which Theo almost did get shot. But that crisis was narrowly averted and the lucky hound lived to fight another day. The masked man was picked up a few days later, and justice served.

Terror is easy to spot. Your body announces terrors arrival with a racing heart, churning stomach, shallow rapid breathing and a ghastly metallic taste in your mouth. It's your biological reaction to staring down the possibility of your own extinction.

The face of fear that trips me up though is the one that grows inside my own mind. It's that voice telling me about the perils and pitfalls of the journey upon which I am embarking, so hard to distinguish from my own rational voice of reason because it sounds so much like it. But this voice is an imposter - a very talented, skilled, clever trickster which has the ability to completely convince me that I'm taking an unrealistic risk. It tells me that I should wake up to myself and quietly sit back down in the corner; to stop pursuing this nonsense and then everything will be alright.

I'm learning to spot her though, this voice. I've discovered I can identify her, address her, and move forward if I handle her in the right manner.

Alan and I recently made the grueling 14 hour flight across the Pacific, which was just one part of the 36 hour-plus transit to Canada. A couple of weeks before we left, I became aware of a growing sense of dread. I had been furiously putting things in place in our business and home, so that if something happened to me, matters would be taken care of as much as possible. I had updated the emergency folder with all of our current passwords and protocols. All the bills and taxes were paid, paperwork completed, accountants and bank managers informed about our wills and powers of attorney. I even found myself writing a note to our sons in case we didn't come back, telling them how wonderful our lives were as their parents, our pride in them and asking them to look after one another.

What I've learned is this: Fear wants to keep us safe, which isn't always a terrible thing. But it can't distinguish between an oncoming train and the light at the end of the tunnel, so it jumps up and down and tells us to stop right there and get off the tracks because we are in danger of meeting our mortal demise. Predictably, the closer the oncoming train or end of the tunnel gets, the louder and more demanding of our attention Fear becomes. And that's the key - it wants our attention. So these days I have a chat with Fear. Once given some attention, it's happy, it calms down and frees me up to once again enjoy the ride.

Every time someone mentioned our imminent travel, the notion immediately popped into my head. We mightn't come back. Each time I talked about it, or even thought about it, the thought was there. I began waking in the small hours of the morning running over in my mind what still needed to be put in place. And we all know you should never believe the things you tell yourself at 2am, don't we? I began dreading the trip, imagining planes falling from the sky into the Pacific Ocean, car accidents, boats sinking...you name it, I thought of it. It became so consuming that a couple of times I even entertained the idea of cancelling the whole trip.
I started questioning whether this might be some kind of premonition - I've heard so many stories of people getting their affairs in order just before going off and unexpectedly checking out, and I've had episodes of this sixth sense before.

I'm not sure what made me do this, but I stopped, right in the middle of some task I can't even recall. I took a few deep breaths, literally wrapped myself in my own arms, and when I was quiet, gently asked: "Is this a premonition, or is this fear?" I think I have Eat, Pray, Love author Elizabeth Gilbert to thank for a story of a conversation she had with herself once. That in itself must have been simmering away on a backburner in my head for a long time.

It turns out that Fear answered my question. How did I know it was fear? Because it was in my head. When I've experienced a sense of knowing in the past, it's all in my gut - or at the very least my heart, my chest. Instead, this torrent came from my mind. I didn't give it much airtime as I'd already been listening to Fear whisper in my ear for weeks.

Almost unbelievably, I found myself having a conversation with Fear that went a little like this:

"I know you are trying to keep me safe, I really appreciate how hard you work watching for danger and showing me how to stay safe. I also know that the things you are afraid of are entirely possible. Yes, the plane might crash. That does happen. Yes, we might have a terrible car accident. That happens too. And yes, muggings and murders and terrorists are also very real things that we may encounter. I also know that those things are not highly likely to happen. They're vague possibilities. What is highly likely though, is that we will have a wonderful adventure, and I want so very much to live a brave and adventurous life. I'm not going to let you keep me from exploring, discovering, growing and expanding. I promise you that I will be careful and alert. I promise you that I will listen when you see danger, and do what is needed to keep us safe. I promise we won't take foolish risks. We are going, and will have a wonderful time. You can come along - in fact, we need you with us - but you aren't getting the map, and you're not going to be allowed to navigate. OK?"

I didn't think about not coming home again. From that moment, I started getting excited. I also slept soundly from then on - at least until jet lag messed with my circadian rhythms.

I discovered that Fear really only wants our attention. Our acknowledgement. The harder I tried to squash, ignore and make it go away, the louder it became. Once given some attention, it's happy, it calms down and frees me up to once again enjoy the ride.

As a creative person - an artist and writer - I am all too familiar with the voice of Fear. It's shut me down a couple of times, trapped me into believing that what I am creating is inferior at best, a total waste of time and complete rubbish at worst. I have on occasion pushed through and miraculously survived, which enabled me to find the courage to then push through again and again. But it's never without a battle. The closer a creative project moves to being ready to share with the world; the louder Fear gets.

This book has been no exception. Fear questions me, tells me:

"Who do you think you are?"

"None of these ideas are new concepts."

"No-one will even want to read this."

And my personal favourite:

"People will think you're a nut job, completely crazy. Who the hell talks to themselves like this? You really probably need a shrink!"

It takes a little while to realise that this, once again, is Fear talking. As I said, it sounds a lot like my rational, evaluative, rational brain. Once again, the 2am whisperings of Fear crank up. But this time, instead of tossing and turning and listening to it all, I instigate another conversation.

"Thanks for showing up. I know you believe you have something important to protect me from. What is it?"

"You're going to make a fool of yourself and look like an idiot. You're just writing rubbish, and you don't even know what you're talking about."

"Yeah, you might be right. I might look like a fool. But I'll look like a fool who followed a dream and listened to the whisper of her soul; and I think I can live with looking like that kind of fool."

Along comes another promise to listen, another request for Fear's company on this journey and a repeat of the instruction about exactly where it gets to sit in the boat. I also request that Fear remains 'hands off' the navigation equipment. As a result, I'm sleeping soundly in no time at all and later wake ready to carry on - at least until Fear once again needs a reminder of the stated role within this outfit. The one certainty I have though is that Fear will pop up again and again. I've realised that I'll never be without Fear. I'm just hoping that I can mostly be in charge and not the other way around.

Work cited: Elizabeth Gilbert, Eat Pray Love, Bloomsbury Publishing, London, 2006.

Chapter 7

Say no to perfectionism
Saying no can be the ultimate self-care
~ Claudia Black

I can't for the life of me understand why such a tiny little word - two letters and just one simple syllable - is so damned difficult to say. I know it isn't hard for everyone but I'm guessing if this book is in your hand right now, it's quite likely you aren't one of the. I have read that it wasn't meant to be difficult to say no. If it were meant to be hard, they would have given it more than two letters.

Alan and the boys (and more recently, their girls) all tell me that I need to learn how to say it. I have a sneaking suspicion though, that they don't expect me to include them in my group of negative response recipients! I have become a little more skilled at doing it but it would be a big fat lie to tell you that I say no to everything to which I don't want to say yes. But, I have discovered a few strategies that seem to help me move through the compulsion to say yes to every damned thing.

By nature, I'm a giver, and generally speaking, I feel great when I'm helping or caring for another person. Of course, this works in the favour of anyone who may want me to help or give to them because it calls to one of my most fundamental character traits.

And if they are having a hard time or are in need, the word 'no' simply will not form in my mouth.

I have learned though, that sometimes I must put my own needs before those of another person. This requires a degree of commitment to myself and a certain level of valuing myself that I haven't always possessed. However, this can be easier said than done, and especially difficult if you have your own version of Muriel squawking away in the back of your mind. She is endlessly saying that you don't deserve the time or consideration you crave. That you have to give all your love in order to be worthy of another's love, and do everything for someone else to gain their approval and attention.

"Look after other people and you might be worthy of love."

"Do what they ask you and they'll like you."

You know how it goes; it's a familiar tune to anyone who's heard it. Over the years, I've said yes to many things that I could have certainly done without. Perhaps the most memorable of all was the day I found myself driving a back-up vehicle behind a pony club trail ride when I really needed to be curled up alone on my couch grieving for my beloved Grandad whom we'd farewelled just two days earlier. The thing is, I say yes to these things. While my heart was aching and my mind was bitterly complaining, I still agreed.

Or, more accurately, I didn't say no. Effectively, I chose them. In saying yes to one thing, we are choosing to say no to another. Many times over, by obliging someone else, I have been saying no to myself.

Expressing these emotions has made me feel quite uneasy and unwell. Digging back through countless memories of smiling and saying, "Yes, of course" when I should have been saying, "I'm sorry, but not this time" has affected me deeply. The recollection has made me realise the endless ways I have disrespected and mistreated myself, and it feels horrid. As I decide that I don't want to dwell on it for a moment longer, I realise that I have actually made progress. I am still eager to jump to help and care for others, but lately I have begun to take a moment to check in with myself first, asking myself questions such as:

"Do I have the energy this will ask for?"

"What will I have to give up in order to do this?"

"How do I really feel about this?"

"Am I prepared for this?"

"Can I fit this in right now?"

"Do I feel really passionate about this?"

A quick check-in and I decide that consciously choosing feels powerful.

I have discovered a few wonderful speeches to have on standby for those moments when I need to say no, beginning with:

> "Let me have a think about it /check out my calendar, and I'll get back to you."

This one buys you some time, and lets you check in with yourself to weigh up your decision. It also allows your decision to feel like your own choice, and not someone else's.

> "Thanks for asking. What you are doing sounds great and I fully support the idea. I can't help you right now, but I'll be interested to hear how it all goes."

Quite often, the things we are asked to support are actually fabulous projects that we would love to see established. We don't always have to be the ones making them fly though. Sometimes, it has to be enough to offer your moral support and encouragement and maintain a keen interest.

What I really long to say goes along the lines of: "I promised myself recently that I would only say yes to things that I am deeply passionate about, and this isn't one of those things."
The writing of Danielle LaPorte has been hugely helpful to me with this. Essentially, what she suggests is that it's okay to say no. No reasons, no excuses, no drama. Thanks. And no.
Or just be completely honest. This idea simultaneously thrills and terrifies me.

"No, my Granddad passed away and I'm sad. I need to curl up on the couch and cry tomorrow."

Why do I feel as though that would be totally self-indulgent and looked upon as weak? If someone had the courage and vulnerability to tell me that, I would want to drop them off a casserole and call on them next week to see how they were doing.

"Sorry, I can't. I've just wound up a huge project and I'm tired. I was looking forward to a long solitary walk and an afternoon nap before I get back into work next week."

Like I said, it is simultaneously thrilling and terrifying.

The inability to say no when necessary can be one of the surest ways to drift off course. When I began writing, I was going to call this chapter 'Weddings, Parties, Anything' because I recognised that I have said yes to all those things - literally - in my own backyard! This is where things get sticky. I believe in celebrating special occasions. I enjoy a good party. I love knocking up a gathering to honour the people I love and their special moments. I've had lots of practice! Yet I have found myself getting all knotted up and pulling out the TV cabinet to clean the dust and dead insects from underneath it before a 21st birthday party. This was on a night when the guests were to party outside, making it unlikely that their memory might include what lay under my television! I have found myself losing sleep over dirty windows that I knew weren't going to get cleaned before a surprise birthday party - which was to be held after dark anyway. On another occasion, I pulled weeds furiously for hours on end in readiness for a 60th wedding anniversary, leaving myself unable to stand up straight for two days while my group of guests were of such advanced maturity, they could barely see me, let alone my weeds. It's not the weddings and parties that I need to say no to; it's my insane need to appear perfect.

So if you want to get married in my garden, I might even say yes! Last time, it was a great day followed by a fabulous party. The difference next time will be that it probably won't be perfect. From this day forward, I'm saying yes to the fun and a big, hearty 'no' to needing to have it all done to perfection.

Work cited: Danielle LaPorte, The Desire Map, White Hot Press and Danielle LaPorte Inc, Canada 2012.

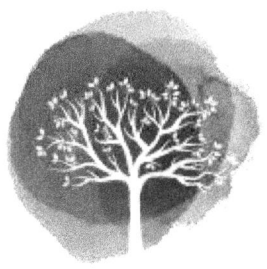

Chapter 8

Compass, maps and harpoon - learning to use your boat's instrument panel

You are far too smart to be the only thing standing in your way
~ Jennifer J Freeman

Our dreamboats come with a bunch of clever navigational tools and really cool accessories fitted as standard issue. Used well, they can help us safely navigate even the most treacherous waters. Perhaps we'll have some rough seas, and we may even become momentarily lost. But if we choose to use our compasses, maps and depth sounders, our chances of safe passage are exponentially greater.

I will explore what I believe some of these instruments to be, along with how I use them or sometimes neglected to use them, and what I have learned from the experience. What I know now is that choosing to use these instruments gets me and my treasure where I want to go faster, more safely and, most importantly, happy and intact.

A combination of these actions, used often and thoughtfully, can give me the course correction I need in life. The key here is the word USED. It's not enough to know this stuff. Not enough to simply acknowledge that these are important habits to weave into our daily routines. We have to choose - and keep on choosing day after day - to invest time and energy into these habits if we hope to experience any benefit. We have to actually do it, not just think about doing it. Not plan to do it. Not even promise to do it. But, actually, really, factually do it.

We'll start by looking at charting our course. How we make plans and use our allotted 24 hours in any given day. We'll think about gratitude, exercise, creativity, mindfulness, boundaries, journaling, acceptance, asking for help and choices. Most of this isn't easy. These actions aren't second nature to many of us but they are actions we need to mindfully and lovingly choose for our own wellbeing.

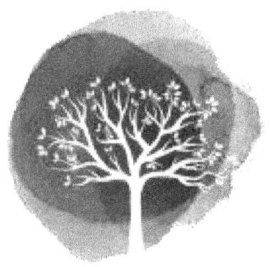

Chapter 9

Chart your course

Only put off 'til tomorrow what you are willing to die having left undone
~Pablo Picasso

Every sailor knows the importance of charting their course and checking that they're on track. No self-respecting mariner would just pick up anchor and set sail without at least checking tide times and familiarising themselves with the voyage route. Obviously, if you jump in your boat and just let the wind blow you at will, you are suddenly at the mercy of the elements (and the pirates!)

I see charting my course as planning and managing my time. The issue here is that time management and I have had an uncomfortable, awkward relationship for many years.

To illustrate this issue, I need to explain that prior to writing this book, my rock star coach Kerrie and I started looking at processes I could use that might assist me to become clearer about what I was going to write and how to achieve that goal. When I made that first call to Kerrie, I had no idea just how far-reaching the results of that conversation would be! It became clear that managing my time had become a thorn in my side (and my foot, and my head and my heart for that matter). From this discussion, we excavated the goal which was to 'have a schedule that frees me'.

When doing my 'Kerrie homework' of clarifying my present and future, I began to contemplate my relationship with time management. I used my art journal to explore this concept, using a sketch of myself juggling madly with so many balls in the air all around me, and many, many balls on the ground that my eyes and hands were anxiously trying to pick up and keep moving. It illustrated how I'd been choosing to handle my life and all of its demands. It still exhausts me to look at this drawing.
To further explain, my natural state is to go with the flow, remaining open to any and all possibilities and never wanting to miss out on an opportunity. I'd like to think it's fluid, easy and fun. The reality though is that it has often ended up in some brand of chaos, with me , stressed and spinning in the middle of it all, accomplishing little. However, I have come to realise that some semblance of order makes life easier and sweeter and saves you wasted hours searching for things for which you have no idea where to begin looking.

Somehow, over many years, my efforts to create order and retain a sense of being open to possibility have evolved into a strange dance of spending a month or two executing elaborate plans with military precision which is followed by four months of struggling to get the most basic functions accomplished on any given day. I always had an ever-present nagging notion that I should be able to do it all if I just tried harder. So, try harder I did. Day planners, written diaries, innovative time management systems, electronic task lists, electronic calendars, wall calendars...you name it, I've tried to make them work for me. Some were effective for getting me to where I was supposed to be when I was supposed to be there - fun places such as the dentist for root canal treatment. But mostly, I felt as though my schedule, in whatever form it took at any given time, was the boss of me. It remained a constant reminder that I wasn't doing enough. I was getting to appointments on time and crossing off jobs, but the stuff I longed to be doing seemed to find its way onto a list and just sit there. It would stay undone until I made a new list to add it to, and another and another, all the while mocking me for not having actually done it. I'd make a plan, and end up beating myself up because even though I'd written it down, I didn't carry it out. All those uncrossed tasks stared back at me as irrefutable evidence that I was a failure.

Yet people around me were saying that they saw me as someone who did so much - who accomplished a lot. But instead of hearing the compliment, Muriel would manage to bring me down, whispering in my ear: "They have no idea how much time you waste. You could be doing so much more!"

It turns out that time management is where my relationship with myself revealed its unhealthy side. But the ah-ha moment I experienced during the journal writing and drawing allowed me the freedom to choose to chart my course in a whole new way. More importantly, it shone a spotlight onto the places I needed to give myself compassion and kindness. The crystal clarity was twofold. It showed me that I can do it all - just not all at once. And I can plan to do it in a way that allows love and compassionate for myself, which, ironically seems to mean that I can in fact get more done. Go figure.

I'm still working on evolving the 'perfect' scheduling technique but I'm fast reaching a point where I might be ready to believe that such a thing doesn't exist.

This is what I have learned about planning, scheduling and time management:

Lesson 1:
    Failing to plan is planning to fail.

I know, I know, it's a catchphrase, but it's true. When you overplan, one day begins to slide into the next, and before long, it's another and another. You get the pressing stuff done and take advantage of the odd opportunity, but the juicy stuff, the important, big, valuable stuff can sit on a shelf for years while you put out all those spot fires. You sash those clothes, pull up the weeds, write the Workplace Health and Safety policy, take the kids to football, pay the bills, brush your teeth, cook dinner and reconcile the accounts. But making the time to spend an hour or two on reflection, getting in touch with your deepest yearnings and then committing to a plan to make them happen is an investment. It's an investment in your own happiness and success and one that offers amazing returns.

Lesson 2:
 There is no right way.

At the moment, I am using a coptic bound book I made in a book binding workshop. I love the weight and feel of it in my hands, it has an assortment of beautiful papers and is completely blank. No printed prompts, no time slots, no calendars. I decided to enjoy taking a couple of hours to add month tabs and calendars, because that's what I do use in a planner. It's now colourful, fun, funky and quite unique. I'm not sure it's the best thing I'll ever use, but so far it's closer than anything else I've tried. I generally dedicate a week to an opening, write the seven days across the top and leave a little room there to add two or three things that are most important on any given day. Right now, I don't have too many commitments that are time-sensitive, so I can manage without the appointment book style of page. Sometimes, I'll pop in an evening meal suggestion there too. I'm a shocker for walking into the kitchen ten minutes before dinner and being surprised that there's no meat defrosted and I've no idea what to cook. I have to confess I always thought meal planning was for people with OCD and nothing better to do with their lives! My apologies to those enlightened people who clearly know much better than I do that a meal plan is a great way to save both money and energy.

It's astounding!

Once I've got the week laid out, and any appointments securely locked in, I start a list. This is where I need to be careful. The temptation to add in 30 tasks, each of which would realistically take two days on their own, is something of which I need to be mindful. I think about my roles and responsibilities. What do I need to address in my business, my family, my creative life, our home? What is getting under my skin, irritating me? How might I address that, or better still, what might I be able to do to remove it altogether? What would simply make me happy, bring me joy? The juiciest thing I can think of goes on the list as a matter of priority.

I choose to keep this list small, a reminder to do the things that would slip through the cracks if I didn't make a commitment to them. The mundane, day to day stuff will always get done. I don't add that to the list, unless I need to feel like a powerhouse of activity and cross off lots of stuff and see my progress In that case, I'll write all that stuff down on a scrap of paper and go nuts with the crossing off for a day or two just to keep that part of my brain satisfied.

My favourite part comes next. I make a couple of appointments with myself. To write or to paint usually, but at least twice a week, there is time set aside in the plan for me to do whatever I am currently being called to create. I resisted the urge to set aside time like this for such a long time. I could always see that it was a good idea, yet I always convinced myself that for some reason or another, it wouldn't work for me. And yet, as with so much of life, all it comes down to is choice. I can choose to make it work or I can choose to keep believing it won't.

Lesson 3:
    Whatever it is that you want has to work for you though, and you alone.

Time management and planners and organisational tools and systems are big business these days. Just Google any of those terms and I'll see you in two weeks when you've still not exhausted the supply of options and systems and tools and programs. This leads me to believe that hopefully I'm not alone in my search for the answer to this confounded problem of fitting in what's expected and what I long for into the 168 hours a week with which we are each blessed. I've realised though, that while we're trying to pour ourselves and our lives and commitments into someone else's concept of effective use of time, we are ignoring the most fundamental, simple truth. We know what we need. We know what we want. Honouring our own integrity and intuition and really listening to ourselves will show us the way, better than any day runner or integrated e-calendar and task list. Ironically, as I write this, I'm considering checking out the Danielle LaPorte Planner for 2016. The email announcing its release just arrived in my Inbox this morning. Might this be the holy grail of time management tools? At the very least, I know it attempts to align with what I'm on about here. Whatever you use, make it your own, and use it in a way that works for you, even if it seems like Swahili to every other soul you know. In this, yours is the only soul that matters.

Lesson 4:
    A schedule is a net for catching days

Or for freeing yourself, like me. Sarah Ban Breathnach introduced me to this concept in her book, Simple Abundance. I believe she's onto something important there. When we make the time to plan our days, we take control of ourselves and our time. A half hour spent looking over the coming week and contemplating our commitments, responsibilities and opportunities gives us the chance to see where things will fit. Put in the 'big rocks first', as Steven Covey so eloquently explained in his book *The Seven Habits of Highly Effective* People so that the rest of the pebbles and sand can slip in around the important stuff (yes, I've used his planners too)!

I know that if I wait for an uninterrupted afternoon or day where I gleefully find myself commitment-free to sink my teeth into some creative work, I'll never even begin. But, if I set aside an hour three times a week, before I know it, there are a few thousand words. In a few months, there's a whole book! Maybe it's not so much that a schedule is a net for catching days, as it is a net for catching time. Which, after all, is what days are made up of.

Lastly, I know that our needs change. Sometimes, I'm constantly planning - checking my planner every day, adding and changing as I juggle the incoming demands of daily life. At other times, the military precision gives way to a loose plan, one that includes the big stuff but seems to have lots of room for whatever might take my fancy. For years, I've berated myself at my lack of consistency. I see now that this is my particular rhythm. For me, life seems to roll across me in waves with a period of busy demands followed by a time of relative quiet. This occurs over and over in a cycle. Sometimes, I am a powerhouse of energy and movement and seem able to move mountains. At other times, I feel the need to regroup, recalibrate and take a few deep breaths. Finally, I understand and am comfortable with both. The thing to remember is to always hold a space to devote time to the important things.

Relationships, with others and ourselves, are what supports and nourishes us. They are what we need to bring joy, beauty, kindness and happiness to the world. Tending to our health and wellbeing, laughing and playing, are things that our so-called 'civilised' Western society tell us we should be too busy for. But they are the very things our souls crave. This is why we need to make appointments with ourselves, for these are all the things that protect our treasure.

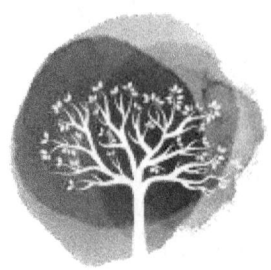

Chapter 10

Savouring every moment

What if you woke up tomorrow with only the things you were grateful for today? ~ Unknown

Ah, good...you're still here. I just ducked off to grab my gratitude journals for reference as I wrote this, and got momentarily waylaid in a tapestry of simple, beautiful moments from my life:

Sitting on the chair swing in the sun, reading a book.

Horses coming up to breathe on the back of my neck as I stop to do some yoga breathing on my morning walk.

Buttery toast with vegemite.

Enormously thankful the snake didn't make it's way into the house through the crack left open in the sliding door!

The boys' stories making me laugh over breakfast.

Sitting at my desk by the window, listening to the social networking of so many birds - Twitter, indeed!

The sunlight lighting up the colours in the glass bottles on my desk.

The reassuring sound of Alan's heartbeat - steady and strong, as my head rests on his chest.

So many perfect moments happen for all of us every day. We wake up, blessed with a fresh new day, and the power to decide how we will approach it. I don't know about you, but pretty soon after that, my mind is flooded with the tsunami of jobs on the agenda: where I need to be, who I need to see, what I have to do. It's all too easy to get caught up in the busyness of this life and race headlong into it, eyes on the next task to cross off the never-ending list and forgetting - in our haste - that magic really is all around us, and we are truly, deeply, wonderfully blessed.

That gratitude was expressed in the weeks after we lost Alan's sister Rae, in an accident. At 54, she was full of life and plans and hopes and dreams and had lots of living to do. She had just that week discovered she was to become a grandmother for the first time. Her kids reflected that she was the happiest they had ever known her to be. Alan and I were at the wedding of a young woman from a family very precious to us when he got the call.

Surrounded by laughter and happiness and the beauty that goes with a wedding, we stood outside the reception, our meals going cold on the table inside as he tried, through his distress, to share the news his father had just told him. I struggled to decipher his words. First of all, I thought he was saying Fraser's name. Then I thought it was Caitlyn and a tractor. No, it's Rae. She was slashing their big yard when the slasher jammed up. She stopped it all and crawled underneath to clear the blockage when the hydraulics let go. The slasher fell across her chest. She's dead.

This news slammed into us - it literally felt as though a truck had hit my chest. As Alan tried to compose himself, I began to shake. I'm still astounded at the intensity of the physical sensation and reaction. Even writing it now, six years later, I still feel it.

We were seven hours' drive away from our kids (young men, but still our kids) and just as far from his parents. We'd both had a couple of drinks celebrating with the newlyweds, so driving that night was not a sensible option. And there was the rather significant matter of a wedding reception that we had just slipped out of which was filled with the friends most precious to us in the world celebrating one of the happiest days in their lives. My sister Deb and her husband Mike appeared at our sides. All we could think about was that we did not want to infect this happy occasion with our sudden sorrow. Somehow we negotiated the next couple of hours of making phone calls and rejoining the reception for a short while.

It's probably unnecessary to say that the week that followed was tough. That pain in our chests refused to budge as we did what needed to be done and waited for the funeral, watching Rae's kids and husband and parents face down the greatest horror of their lives.

You might be wondering what the hell this all has to do with gratitude? Well, those tiny savoured moments were what helped to get me through that time. Stopping, if only for a second, to acknowledge that despite the pain in my chest and the spinning in my head, there are blessings to comfort me. I felt desperately sad when I was experiencing all those things, but the simple act of stopping and noticing and taking a second to write them down as things for which I am thankful helped me to get through the extreme sadness.

That is the great irony of practicing gratitude. When you are at your lowest and desperately struggling with the cards that life has dealt, that is the time you need to practice it most. It's easy to feel lucky and thankful and be grateful when things are humming along well, and all your ducks are lining up and good things are rolling your way. The challenge comes at those other times, because it is monumentally difficult to see anything good when your world is in scattered shards at your feet.

I'm not always good at this. I can sink down into that murky place where everything seems grey and cloudy and I tell myself there's not a damned thing for which to be thankful. When that happens, I know it's time to grab a pencil and sheet of paper and make my list of fundamental, basic, every day gratitude's. We can all do this. There will be 100 things for which you can be grateful right now, if you put your mind to it.

Here's a few off my list to get you started:
- I woke up today - plenty of people didn't make it to today
- I am physically able to walk, talk, sing, laugh, cry, stretch and hug another person
- I can see, hear, taste, smell and feel
- I have a roof over my head and a safe place to sleep (in fact, I have a home I adore)
- I have a husband, sons, daughters-in-law, grandchildren who love and support me and are a source of joy and fun
- I have a handful of the best friends the world ever knew
- I never have to feel hungry
- I have clean clothes hanging in a cupboard
- I have a quiet place I can go to think and rest
- There is food in my refrigerator
- I have a refrigerator!!
- I can read and learn
- I can write and communicate
- That first cup of tea in the morning
- The smell of rain
- A hot shower
- A quiet glass of wine as the sun sets

Get the idea? I have a friend who often recalls the night she wearily headed to bed, picked up her journal to write what she was grateful for. Her husband was in the throes of an affair and her marriage and life were in tatters. She sat on the bed, desolate, and then wrote:

I am thankful for the hum of the dishwasher. I don't have to stand there and wash up those dishes.

The stuff we often take for granted is where the power of gratitude lies.

The real power though lies in the 'practice' part. It's the act of stopping to acknowledge and record your moments of thankfulness that gives you traction. My intention is to practice gratitude daily. My reality is that I often don't manage that. I've been 'practicing' on and off for long enough to see and know there is a difference. Oprah Winfrey is just one of the many high profile people who espouse the value of keeping a gratitude journal. It seems to me that there are lots of ways you can carry out gratitude practice. A journal, preferably a beautiful blank book dedicated to the purpose, is probably my 'go to' practice. A Happiness Jar, which you fill with slips of paper recording one thing each day that has made you smile, is another way. Prayers of thanks are gratitude. Handwritten thank you cards are gratitude. Looking up and saying thank you when you narrowly avoid dicing your finger with that sharp knife while slicing onions for dinner is gratitude.

Committing to a practice - whether it's writing one thank you note a day to someone who has touched your life or scribbling off five things at the end of every day that you are grateful for - has an interesting effect. I've noticed it again and again. Once you begin to regularly document your gratitude, your brain begins to look for things. Almost as if it's thinking "Geez, I have to think of five things to write about again tonight, I better pay attention!" Miraculously, you begin to notice more and more for which to be thankful:

The kind, friendly smile from the girl at the supermarket.

The loveliness of the sunlight as it filters through lace curtains blowing in the breeze. The twinkle of fairy lights (one of my personal favourites).

The unexpected phone call from an old friend.

Freshly painted toenails.

A clean home.

Fresh sheets on the bed.
The bank account reconciliation balancing first go (this one makes me fist-pumpingly happy!

Today, on top of all the things I am thankful for every day, I am thankful for some undisturbed time to write, for my sister, who happens to be my best friend, for a conversation with Alan that illuminated something I had never connected before, for my health and for the energy I feel for what I'm writing here. I notice that my gratitude journal has a lot of empty pages, and find myself thankful for the possibility of all the special little moments with which I will eventually fill it.

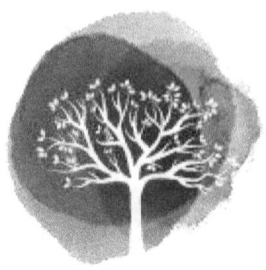

Chapter 11

Quit being so damned busy
Beware the barrenness of a busy life ~ Socrates

There's so much to do. I'll never get through all this. I'm so busy. I just don't have time...

Enough already. Yes, it's true that it's the end of the financial year and I leave on my holiday in four weeks. Before then, I need to have our financial stuff all processed, copied, filed and off to the accountant, the PAYG summaries submitted to the tax office, the BAS paid and the bank review signed off. We also need to fit in a trip to Brisbane, pack for a month in Canada, mow the lawn, clean the fridge out, do the washing, make the four hour round trip to the physio for this dinky hip, write six chapters of a book, do a blog post a week... And, and, and - for the love of Pete (who is Pete by the way and why should we love him?) Stop. Breathe. Look around, the sun is shining, it's a glorious day, you are blessed with a healthy, wonderful family, you have a handful of amazing friends, you are healthy. You will not get all of that done today. It's entirely possible you may not get all of that done in four weeks. Then again, you just might. But sure as tomorrow's Tuesday, you will not get it all done at once, and you certainly won't get it all done by freaking out about it. It's also utterly, unequivocally definite that you won't get it done by telling anyone else how busy you are.

It's tempting to live on that dangling rope...swinging around at its unravelling end, clinging for dear life to the notion that if you just keep pushing you'll get 'er done. Don't rest, don't stop, push push, push and you'll win.

Wrong.

I know this. I know it so well, it sickens and embarrasses me. I know this won't work, because I tried this exact technique for years. It gets you places alright. It gets you sobbing into a friend's lap. It gets you very uncomfortably into your doctor's rooms being prescribed anti-depressants. It gets you a hospital bed and a heart monitor. You'd think that one trip to bedrock would have been all it should take to wise up. But no - it seems that I am an excruciatingly slow learner, and I'm not entirely sure how many times I made it to rock bottom before the lesson really sank in.

The most recent visit to the bottom rocked me because I promised myself I'd never go there again. That I knew now what caused the fall and I would avoid it. I avoided it alright. I avoided it so well that instead of developing the symptoms of anxiety I was familiar with, I managed to create some new ones, thereby fooling myself into thinking it was something else entirely.

My old friend Muriel was on fire, too. She berated me endlessly, and when she realised I had broken a promise to myself, holy cow, did she turn up the volume. Here's the thing: a promise to yourself is the most tender, precious and important of all promises. They're also the ones we break first. After all, no-one knows except us, right? We tell ourselves it doesn't matter because no-one else knows we broke that commitment. But we know. Every time we dishonour a commitment we make to ourselves, part of us withers. Do it often enough, and our souls start to feel like hard, shrivelled, nasty little nuggets. It is, I've come to believe, an insidious form of self harm. There's no physical evidence, no outward signs, just us, growing even more empty and distrusting of our own selves.

I'm reasonably sure I'm not alone in getting so caught on the roundabout of 'too busy' that I've unintentionally caused myself hurt and harm by denying the necessary and simple actions which nourish and renew me.
The irony of it is that when I finally wised up and began to make sure I chose to take the time for half an hour of yoga, 10 minutes of meditation, an afternoon with a friend or whatever it might be on any given day that renews me; I started to accomplish more. Hang on? What? Spending less time on the list of jobs, but crossing more off? Trying less, achieving more? Relaxing more, enjoying more and doing more? Yes. Bizarrely, somehow that's how it works. The less I stress and push and strain; the easier it gets.

There are lots of people in this world who I fear may die by their own 'so busy' sword. I'm sure you know at least one of them. Every encounter leaves you feeling drained, having listened to a torrent of how busy they've been, how busy they are right now, how busy they are going to be, and there's no end to the busyness in sight! A sage and gentle soul I know once suggested that these people are no busier than the rest of us - they just seem to find the time to tell us about it.

We live in a world where busy has become a badge of honour. I'm sorry, but a script for Zoloft and most of a day in a hospital enduring a Cardiac Stress Test doesn't seem all that honourable to me. However, a life full of beauty and fun and adventure and richness? Now, that I want to sign up for. How many of the Busy Brigade view their days this way? All that 'busy', if we choose, can be beautiful and fun and adventurous and rich. It's all about our attitude.

I have a chalkboard in our living area upon which I like to write a good quote. Right now, it bears these words, first uttered by Bob Bitchin:

"The difference between an adventure and an ordeal is attitude."

It isn't always easy, and I certainly don't always manage to embrace a positive attitude; but what I do know for sure is that most experiences in our lives are greatly influenced by the attitude we choose to bring. Our attitude is OURS to choose. Sometimes it takes everything we have to choose the positive attitude. Like that boozy Christmas party you don't want to go to, but your hubby has been looking forward to for weeks. You can grumble and mutter, and drag yourself along; your head full of things you could be doing if you didn't have to be here, and you'll have a predictably shitty time. OR you can choose to dress yourself in something that makes you feel good, whack on some bright lippy and decide to set yourself a challenge to mentally note one positive, desirable quality about everyone in the room. Bright lippy, in case you didn't know, is scientifically proven to improve your mood. Okay, so I'm not sure about the scientific part, but I am sure it's effective! And you know what? I'll bet once you start focusing on the good stuff, you'll notice more good stuff, and you might even catch yourself having a good time. It's all about choosing your attitude.

My little stint on the treadmill, hooked up to leads and heart monitors led me to decide it was time to change my attitude towards busy. It took a bit of digging and soul-searching, and a major shift in my thinking, but it's working. It saw me move from trying to do it all, today, preferably before lunch, with a smile on my face and perfection at every turn to realising that I might be able to do it all, but I'm damned well never going to get it all done at once. I have realised that trying to do too much is a surefire path to misery and self-hatred. You set yourself up to fail from the beginning if you try to do it all; expect to do it perfectly and forget that you are, after all, only human.

The resulting art journal page of me juggling all those bloody balls (and dropping many of them) was created. It's far from the most stunningly beautiful artwork I've ever done. In fact, as a drawing, technically, it's pretty ordinary and that's being kind! But what that exercise unlocked in my mind was monumental. Suddenly, the answer was crystal clear to me.

Then came the 'how I want to be' vision: calm, centred, focussed and steady. And do you know what? I asked myself "Is it possible that you are trying to do too much?" and the answer was "That's a fucking stupid question!" Of course I am!" Ever since that day, something has shifted in me. The reality which I have long understood academically, I finally understood in my heart and my gut.

I then decided to write this sweet, but clear note to myself:

No amount of planning and scheduling is going to put more hours in a day or make you into some kind of time-bending superhero. Sweetie...you have to choose. You have to decide. What do you really want in the schedule, and what can go? You cannot do it all...

I'm not going to tell you that I never get swept up in 'busy' any more. Old habits die hard, as they say. BUT, I catch it quick. I notice the constriction in my chest and the dull ache behind my eyes. And I stop, take five to breathe deeply and recalibrate. Because this life is precious. It's a wonderful, miraculous gift. The world has aardvarks and rainbows and polar bears and canyons and tiny little birds and enormous rocks in the middle of deserts and beauty and wonder that would blow our minds if only we stopped long enough to take it in. But instead, we wrestle with deadlines and hurry through our days, only to fall, depleted, into bed so we might have the energy to get up and hurry again tomorrow. I'm utterly certain that this is not how we are supposed to live.

The world has it's tragedies and darkness, I know. Lord, I know. The six o'clock news is often enough to leave me wanting to go and hide under the bed indefinitely. Then I remember how long it is since I vacuumed under there, and imagine the hay fever attack, and it doesn't feel like a safe bet anymore. It's safe to say that there are at least a thousand things we could be broken- hearted about every hour. But, will feeling shattered and heartbroken make the reality any easier for anyone to bear? Will it change anything for anyone? Of course not. However, making the time to acknowledge the beauty and the wonder that does exist just might. If we can bring ourselves to the world filled with a sense of wonder and appreciation and beauty; that might just be infectious enough to seep into the souls of others.

So I urge you, for heaven's sake, stop choosing relentless busyness. We all have lots to do. That's life. It's a given. Let's just get on with it, and while we're at it, take five minutes here, half an hour there, to share something beautiful and real with our partners, our kids, our friends, even the sour girl at the supermarket. Share a meal with people you love, phones turned off, giving one another the beautiful gift of our rapt attention. Take a walk and stop to watch that soaring eagle, or wee little insect building it's intricate nest. Get outside and lay in the grass, finding elephants and ice creams in the clouds drifting by. Choose beauty over busy for a moment or two every day. You'll be astonished what a difference it can make.

Work cited: Quote by Bob Bitchin from his website bobbitchin.com

Chapter 12

Do the Downward Facing Dog
I bend, so I don't break.
~Unknown

I know, I know... You don't want to. God knows, I don't want to either. It's possible that I have come close to making an artform out of avoiding exercise. I hate to sweat. I hate huffing and puffing for breath even more. That endorphin rush runners talk about? Bullshit. It just hurts. And don't even get me started on the discomfort endured when the E cup boobs bounce up and down on my chest! There has been no sports bra created that can stop the effect of gravity and motion on large areas of breast tissue. I know this. I have parted with way too much hard-earned cash in the quest to acquire the perfect support for the girls, all to no avail.

It would be safe to say I hate exercise. I actively avoided it for many years. When our boys were small, I got plenty of it chasing them. In fact, I can recall my father suggesting to me that I could use a little more meat on my bones at a time when my days consisted of running between catastrophes created by small people.

Our boys were busy. The world was one enormous bucket of fascination to them, to be explored, examined, dismantled and conquered - preferably before morning tea time. Every damned day. A three day old puppy was found choking in the toilet bowl -

the toilet cleaner no doubt burning it's tiny, delicate, respiratory tract. Somehow it survived! Scrambled eggs were cooked by a three and a half-year-old Keelan - chair pulled up to the cooktop - accompanied by the announcement that "Scrambled egg with honey doesn't taste very good, Mum."

One son with hairdressing aspirations took to his head with scissors close to the scalp, on either side of his head, advising me "That's where my horns are going to grow." I kept a close eye on those spots for horn buds... it seemed entirely possible that horns might sprout at any moment! Fin had a thing for scissors, having sometime earlier cut right through the power cord of an overlocker which was plugged in and turned on. To this day, I cannot fathom how that didn't electrocute him. It blew a chunk out of the scissor blades... I can only be eternally grateful to the brilliant individual who came up with plastic grips on scissors. And fate. Fate was kind to us that day, I think.

Fraser attempted to abseil off the verandah, wearing a pair of jocks and a pushbike helmet; a piece of rope tied in a very dodgy knot around his waist, which was all that existed to save him from a sudden thud as he swung over the railing.

They started walking at nine months old, climbing at nine and a half months, and running by ten. Our washing line looked like a tiny bullfighter's laundry was hung there after I quickly discovered that red shirts were the easiest to spot from a distance. That was very helpful when they took off at a gallop, having climbed the fence, toppled over the top and crashed to the ground; only to jump up, unscathed, and head as fast as they could to the nearest shed, vehicle, animal or (on a lucky day) interesting adult. It wasn't so bad when there was just one. But by the time there were three of them, all trying to outdo one another for the day's greatest adventure award, I was in constant motion and generally eight steps behind the game.

They were a great team too. Together, they managed to fill the floor of our sedan with water from a hose while at a birthday party one time. I'll never forget the withering look of the woman who came to tell me what they were doing. Part of me was impressed as I had only checked on them about 90 seconds earlier. How the hell did they even manage it?!

Standing around chatting after Alan's brother's family bull sale one day, I noticed his Dad's ute starting to move backwards and I started running. In that ute were our three boys and their cousin Lisa. There were probably about 60 or 70 other cars all parked there, on a slight slope. Fortunately, the ute was rolling backwards the way it had been parked, and managing to avoid other parked cars so far. As I got alongside it, there they were, four children screaming in fear of their lives as I try to keep my balance, run alongside the car and open the door. The next challenge was to get them to scoot over so I could slide in and reach the brake. This was made difficult by the fact they wouldn't stop screaming. I never was sure if they were screaming out of fear of being hurt by the car running into something, or by their grandfather when he got hold of them!

Clearly, I had little need of exercise for at least 10 to 15 years while the boys were growing up. As it happens though, those little boys grew into young men, and eventually became wonderful company and great fun to be around. And, I stopped running. The reduction in sudden heart-thudding drama was good for me or so I thought for a while. But I guess the somewhat more sedentary nature of my days slowly began to tell on me. Where was all that energy I had when they were small? Oh hang on - maybe that was just pure adrenalin I was getting by on. The need for some form of regular movement started out as one of those things I knew I should do, because, well, all those news reports about cancer and heart disease and diabetes and insomnia and depression and parasite infestations all finish off with "eat a healthy diet and get plenty of exercise." Okay, maybe not the parasite infestations. But you know what I mean. Everyone, everywhere seems to know that exercise is awesome. And they seem to enjoy it. As for me - I'd rather have a root canal.

There were a couple of half-hearted attempts at embracing this exercise thing. I may have even purchased a 'workout' video. At least 27 times, I decided I was going to walk every day - you know, that power walking kind of walk. The boob bounce isn't as awful when you walk, as opposed to running. This idea would last approximately a day and half, on average. Then I read Sarah Ban Breathnach's book *Simple Abundance*, in which she talks about walking not as exercise, but as something akin to a moving meditation. This notion appealed to my stubbornly resistant brain, and I became an appreciator of the long walk. The walk on which you breathe, and engage all your senses in being in the world. The ramble during which you stop to rest on a fallen log by the lagoon, and watch the pelicans and ducks dive for whatever tasty morsel hangs out in the pond scum on the bottom of the dam. The walk which is not for exercise's sake, but for sanity's sake. This kind of walk has become one of my favourite things. Not every day. Not even once a month. Which is great for my sanity and sense of peace, but still doesn't qualify as exercise.

I have always enjoyed a good stretch. So, when a friend encouraged me to go along and try a yoga class, I was a little more inclined to try that than many exercise options suggested to me in the past.

It only took one class.

This was it. This is my exercise. I walked out of that first class feeling so juicy and wonderful and calm and alive all at once. (Melody, if you're reading this - thank you. That yoga class seriously altered the very trajectory of my existence.) Over time, I discovered that yoga can make you grunt and sweat and even huff and puff. I even love it when I'm red- faced and breathless.

Over time, I noticed things. I noticed that I sleep more soundly and peacefully when I've been practicing yoga regularly. It also seems true for walking or even some good old- fashioned energetic gardening. Doing something physical helps you rest well. I'm sure there are all kinds of scientific evidence to support that - I'm just going on the evidence of my own body. I noticed that I became calmer and better able to weather the storms of life. Like the tree pose, where you 'put roots down through your grounded foot, while at the same time opening up and out'. Steady and strong on the ground, while simultaneously flexible and fluid on top.

Every so often you are asked to try to get into a pose that initially has you thinking "Yeah. Sure. My foot is never gonna meet my hand there." But, almost miraculously, you discover it will, which has a remarkable effect on your faith in yourself and your body. Your confidence grows. Your trust in yourself and your body expands just a little more. And the stretch feels amazing.

None of this is to suggest that yoga is for everyone. My daughter-in-law Leah can't bear the thought. "Boring!" She has an appreciation for sweating, shaking knees and burning lungs. My friend Shelley is religious in her devotion to jiu jitsu. She rolls around on the floor with her opponent's sweaty armpits in her face and loves it. I know plenty of perfectly sane normal people who love to run - for miles and miles. They all say the same things:

> It's my time for me.
> It's when I get to clear my head.
> I just tune everything else out for an hour.
> It keeps me sane.

Finally, I get it. It's not so much about being fit and toned and weighing a particular number, although I know those things can certainly be important motivators for some people. It's about engaging in an activity which affirms our commitment to ourselves. Devoting time to our own wellness - physical and mental - is a powerful way to say to ourselves: "I love you, I appreciate you and I want to take care of you. You are important and you deserve some time spent on you to help you feel good."

I plan to be getting my Downward Facing Dog pose on every day for the rest of my life. I just need to train Alan to be a little more careful about the way in which he might bring the truck driver in for an early morning coffee - while I'm hanging upside down, butt in the air, braless, in my pyjamas; gazing up between my knees to greet him!

Work cited: Sarah Ban Breathnach's Simple Abundance, Hodder and Stoughton - Hodder Headline Aust. Pty. Ltd. Sydney 1995

Chapter 13

Channel your inner Picasso

Every child is an artist, the problem is how to remain an artist once he grows up. ~ Pablo Picasso

By nature, I'm not a terribly organised person. When the boys were small, there were other mothers around me talking about routines - bathtimes, bedtimes, nap times, meal times, snack times, playtimes - I was thrilled if I managed to get out of my pyjamas and comb my hair some time during the course of the day! I would beat myself up because I was certain that those other mums were never vacuuming at 5pm, and I knew they never left the nappies on the clothesline overnight. But, looking back, I realise that sitting on the floor with the kids for hours on end doing that jigsaw puzzle of all those damned silly koalas on the beach was in fact more than acceptable. I beat myself up about not being on top of the housework and having an ironing pile bigger than Mount Kilimanjaro (Hell, I still have an ironing pile bigger than Mount Kilimanjaro!) and 'wasting' time making play dough, finger painting and having some fun with my little ones when I 'should' have been organised and all Suzy Homemaker.

But I was smarter than I knew. Those kids grew so fast, and I'll wager that they don't recall whether their jocks hung on the clothesline for three days or made it directly back into their drawers by lunch time on washing day. What I hope they remember is walking to the billabong, reading stories and building cubbies in the kitchen that their mum let them leave there for a week at a time. Those cubbies drove me nuts. But, even then, I knew that making something and exploring and creating were important. It's a need that I believe every human being possesses. To breathe life into something that, without us, and our own unique being, wouldn't exist in the world.

I have a passionate belief in the transformative power of creativity. I believe that an almost primal human urge is to bring into being something that would not exist without us. In response to my own acts of creativity, I'm often told by others that: "I'm just not creative" or "I don't have a creative bone in my body." But I disagree. Perhaps I have some skill - but it has been developed over time with practice, play and more epic messy failures than I care to admit. Perhaps this is something which you haven't yet tapped into for yourself. Don't even get me started on the "I can't draw a straight line" comment. Neither can I! That's what they made rulers for, dammit! I believe that if you can hold a pencil (even if it's with your toes) you can draw. You may hate your first attempts. You may need some guidance. You may need to retrain your brain to really see the things you are looking at. But, with a little time and an open mind, you could draw. I promise.

Humans make stuff. In fact, humans make awesome stuff. I mean, the world has astonishing creations like the ancient Pyramids of Giza, the statue of David, and coat hangers. (Really, how clever was the dude (or dudette) who made coat hangers?) There are songs, movies, paintings, books, gardens, clothes, furniture and so much beauty in the world, because someone, somewhere, felt the call to create.

We can all make stuff. I create paintings, take photos and write stories. I know amazing souls who make quilts, beautiful photos and music that touches our souls. There are endless ways to be creative, and I am certain that deep within every one of us lies a longing to live creatively, a longing to bring our unique, authentic selves to our everyday lives. Some people create incredible meals and their kitchen is akin to their church. Although I'm open to any invitation to taste test, the kitchen isn't my happy place.

Others fascinate and mystify me with their ability to breathe lush, flourishing life into soil, conjuring gardens where weeds were all that once grew. My gardening skill is pretty much limited to the understanding that it should be planted with the green bit pointing up, and there is probably supposed to be some water added at some point! There are those who design homes, whole buildings even! The list could go on and on. Creativity can extend to imagining a new way to perform a routine task, or an expanded view of a problem that shows the way to a clever solution.

One of the things I've enjoyed most in this lifetime is teaching art journalling classes. Art journalling can be defined in many different ways, depending on who is defining it. For me, it is the intersection of keeping a written diary and a sketch book, with the addition of lots of colour, and complete abandonment of any attachment to a finished product. It's a 'just for me' activity which sometimes yields brilliant pieces of art. It also sometimes yields puddles of muddy colours and scribbles and scratchings that aren't the slightest bit remarkable. But it doesn't matter, because the only purpose it really ever had to serve was to get a feeling or thought out of my head and onto the page, in order to be transformed. Which is exactly what happens. Every time - no matter what the resulting page looks like.

That is the magic of creation. You begin with a head full of thoughts and a heart full of feelings.

Even if what you are making has absolutely nothing to do with those thoughts and feelings, the act of creating while holding those things in your mind and heart somehow transforms them. A traumatic experience, a sorrow, an irritation, a loss, a delight, even a great excitement, are all filtered through with your own uniqueness colouring and showing itself in the thing you've made. Even though I give my art journalling groups the same materials and lesson on technique, by the end of the session we have many beautiful pages - every one of them completely different. We are simply unable to make a thing without something of ourselves showing up in it. It's the reason our handwriting is different from everyone else's, it's the way you can often guess who brought along a particular dish for your pot luck dinner. Sadly, we all too often look at the creative offerings of others and wish ours looked more like that. What we often don't know is that others are looking at our offerings and wishing theirs were more like ours. One of the early sessions in our art journalling class looks at introducing handwriting - not only as a form of expression but also as an illustrative tool. The lament "But I have awful handwriting!" quickly arises. But it's YOURS - it's a special part of you, like your nose or your eyes or your toes or your soul. We are so very quick to dismiss ourselves as not being good enough for endless different reasons. Really, we should be loving the hell out of the fact that we get to be here (making stuff) at all!

In her research on shame, vulnerability and wholeheartedness, Brene Brown discovered that a critical component of wholeheartedness is creativity (trust me, if you're unfamiliar with her work, it's time you changed that!). As she says: "If we want to make meaning, we need to make art." Art doesn't have to be a gallery-worthy painting. It might be a shell wind chime, a hand-knitted scarf, a scrapbook page, a junk sculpture, a vegetable garden or a dance. In my experience, this is clearly true. When we create, we connect seemingly unrelated things. And we make sense of our world and our experiences as we see those connections.

If I had taken the time to document every artwork I've created, I could tell you endless stories of the connections and clarity I've discovered during their creation. Lucky for you, all that remains is the artwork. The emotions and mental gymnastics that accompany the creative journey dissipate and ultimately disappear as the creative work evolves. It's as if the paint and paper absorbs the thoughts and feelings, digests them, turns them into something positive and often beautiful, and reflects that back to me - regardless of what was poured in by me in the first place. The resulting pieces say something to me for which there are no words.

I once donated an artwork to a local fundraising dinner, which was to be auctioned during the course of the evening. I should have been prepared and known the auctioneer would need something to say about the piece as he put it up for auction. If I'd been asked what mediums I'd used, or how I'd created it, I could have answered that in a flash. But the question asked was "What is it about?" Do you know, to this day, I struggle to articulate what that painting is about. At the time I floundered for a good while, asked to have a few minutes to write something down, hoping the clarity I was searching for might come more readily through writing. It didn't. I handed that poor man some garbled, odd explanation that I don't believe he even used. I couldn't blame him.

The thing upon which I found myself reflecting most deeply though was how very uncomfortable I felt being directly questioned: "What does it mean?"

Initially, my response was that while I may have something in mind as I created the piece, what was important to me was for each individual to experience their own response to it. I hoped the viewer would interpret the piece in their own way and find their own unique meaning within it. I felt almost irritated that I was being interrogated and forced to 'explain' it in great detail.

I later realised that the poor man was probably feeling a bit out of his depth, his auctioneering experience in the past heavily weighted to property, cattle and items of which he no doubt had a greater understanding and knowledge. He was just trying to get some information to help him do the job well. I must say that he did do well, despite my fumbling for an explanation. I later dwelled on my feelings of discomfort and difficulty in expressing the artwork's meaning. Then it struck me - if I could put it into words, I'd be able to write it, not paint it! It's a feeling, it's broad and deep and powerful, and in my heart I know exactly what it means, but I struggle to put words around it. That is why we need to create - it enables us to give form to something that is essentially impossible to pin down, to process thoughts and feelings that sit just below the surface of our ability to name and express them merely with words. Interestingly enough, the title of that piece is 'Soul's Search for Home'. It is not lost on me that many years later, I am writing this book, and finding the words I was searching for back then.

In a nutshell, creating something can take a negative experience and transform it into something beautiful. It can tenderly cradle a positive experience and cement that joy and beauty into a tangible touchstone.

I put my belief that everyone is creative in some way or another to the test when I put together a project for our local River Festival. Inspired by a similar idea carried out in the regional Queensland town of Roma, we called it "Leonardo, are you living in Theodore?" A dozen people - none of whom believed themselves to be artists, or even particularly creative - were sent a 12-inch canvas with a letter explaining that I believed they possessed some untapped talent and that I'd love for them to 'have a go' at creating an artwork based on the theme of Water. I would have been pleased if half of those approached had taken up the challenge. But to my delight, all but one finished and delivered their creations. They painted, paper maiched, collaged, drew, sculpted and shared with the world a total of 11 incredibly diverse, deeply meaningful artworks. I offered to provide a space, access to art supplies and a little technical expertise for anyone who wanted some assistance. Some took me up on that offer. Watching them move through the process from being nervous and uncertain to becoming completely absorbed in breathing life into their creation, to the obvious delight when they felt their piece was complete, was a tremendous joy.

These 11 brave souls are, to me, proof positive that with a little encouragement and support, and a lot of courage, we can create things that not only bring meaning for ourselves, but also touch others. Without exception, they told me enthusiastically "That was actually a lot of fun!" Hearing afterward that a couple of them had taken themselves off and purchased some art supplies so they could continue to explore their creativity made my heart soar.

At the time, although I believed in them, I was surprised that so many of those asked to participate actually embraced the idea. But I think it's because there is an innate need in all of us to create. Perhaps we don't seem to have room or time for creativity in our lives, but somewhere inside, we all have a four-year- old just longing to crack open that new box of crayons, sprawl out on the floor for hours and create the life of our dreams on 28 sheets of butcher's paper.

People tell me that time is the number one barrier preventing their creative urge. At least, it's a lack of time which they blame. I'll let you in on a little secret. I almost choke on my own bile when people say "I wish I had time to do that." Time and again, I am asked in incredulous tones: "How do you find the time? It's as though I may have somehow found a loophole in the Universal Law of time that issues each of us with exactly 168 hours a week.

For years, I walked away from those conversations feeling as though I was cheating, flaking off, or simply not taking life seriously enough if I could be finding time to be creative. Here's another little secret - I make time. I choose. I've already alluded to the state of my ironing pile! If you wait until you have time, it won't happen - we'll never have time! But if you make time, it can happen.

Even if you can only manage 10 minutes a day before everyone else gets up or an hour in the evening instead of watching that inane reality TV show; little bites of time gradually add up to completed sketches, whole chapters, and finished scarves.

More importantly, what it adds up to is you feeling whole because you've listened to your soul when it's whispered to you: "We need to create something."

Work cited: Brene Brown, The Gifts of Imperfection, Hazelden, Minnesota, 2010

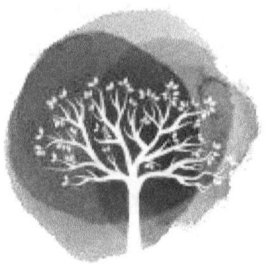

Chapter 14

Find your soulful self
The quieter you become, the more you can hear
~ Ram Dass

Whatever you want to call it, and to whichever mode of spirituality you wish to subscribe, the important thing is that there is some kind of connection in your life with the Divine, Spirit, the Universe, God, Allah, Buddha or all those dudes together, if that's your way.

I was raised by a self-confessed fallen Catholic and an atheist. My mum's parents were devout Catholics who went to Mass every Sunday, ate fish on Friday and partook in Confession, Hail Marys and Holy Water. The full Catholic commitment. Dad called himself an atheist, but enjoyed discussing the Holy Book so much with the Mormons who occasionally visited, they deigned him ready for baptism! I'm not sure that atheist is really the right description for my Dad - but that's another story, for another time.

As a child, I spent many happy Sundays alongside my Nana and Grandad in Church. The ceremony and ritual felt somehow comforting to me. I embraced it all to such an extent that for a time, Mum and Dad believed I would grow up to become a nun. I don't recall ever having any aspirations in that direction, and I think they were both relieved when that apparent passion waned. Somewhere along the way, I came to understand that simply showing up to church and saying the prescribed number of Hail Mary's after confession did not a Christian make. I had an Aunt who was married to a man from a 'Good Catholic Family'. He was one of, if memory serves correctly, nine siblings, and was the exception to his family being full of priests and nuns. He would tell you he was a good Catholic, a good Christian. When I learned that he would take his family home after Sunday Mass and beat his pregnant wife, my young and impressionable mind slammed the book closed on organised religion. If THAT is what good Christians do - I wanted no part of it.

A connection with Spirit though, I did want. The belief in something bigger than us, in the inexplicable, has stayed with me. Meditation and I go way back. And, just like old, true friends, we can go years without seeing one another and then one sweet day, pick up just where we left off. When I was pregnant with Fin - as a young woman of around 25 - Alan and I went off to a weekend retreat kind of thing called Alpha Dynamics. Looking back, I'm fascinated that I persuaded him to go - it's so not his thing - and wonder how we afforded it. It's one of those classic cases of decide you're going to do it, and work out later how you'll make it work. Clearly, it did work out. Almost 30 years later, looking back, I am deeply grateful for the experience at that point in my life. I am also deeply grateful for Alan being there with me. During the intervening years, I think he may have meditated exactly zero times, but he went along largely because he gets it and he gets me. God love him; so much of what happens in my head is like Swahili to him, yet he still somehow arranges his mind to make space for the possibilities of Swahili. Of all the things I struggle to articulate, my fascination and appreciation for the way he gets me, even though he doesn't get it, is the most difficult.

The Alpha Dynamic lingo referred to it as 'going to your levels' - the Alpha brainwave being the desired level of consciousness. Over time, I came to understand the process as meditation, then mindfulness; and I realised that there is no right or wrong way to practice this just as there is no right or wrong way to do anything. There is only the way that works for us, which finds results. Other people might recognise this as prayer. What we call it is not anywhere as important as doing it.

Some days I'm a meditating rock star - having all kinds of almost psychedelic visions and surges of wonderful bubbliness buzzing through my physical self. Other days, it feels impossible to stop the orangutans in my mind from shrieking and swinging through my pointless preoccupations, slinging shit as they go. Yet, even an orangutan-filled meditation is better than no meditation at all. Afterwards, I feel calmer, more patient, more tolerant and more cheerful. I find a beautiful sense of expanded possibility and optimism.

Yet, I can forget about all that amazing positive sensation and just choose not to mediate today, this week, this month. It's back to the age-old and battle weary excuses of: "Too much to do," "Not enough time today," "I'll do that after I've…(pick your own trip wire here - finished the bookwork, put dinner on, made this phone call, mowed the lawn, answered that email, picked the lint out of my navel…)" You get the picture.

I find myself wondering why I would choose to leave out one of the activities that brings me the greatest peace and sustenance, and which is completely within my reach and command. Here I am, writing this book about how to live your best life and care for your own wonderful self, and I realise that I've not given myself a yoga session or meditated in the past five days. Excuse me… there's something I need to go and do RIGHT NOW.

Okay. Yes. I needed that. I need it every damned day. For me, that 15 minutes is pretty much the difference between strong and steady, and bat shit crazy. All it takes is 10 or 15 minutes, people! Out of a whole day! It's 10 or 15 minutes to connect with something bigger than ourselves, to become quiet and listen to what the Great

Creator has to tell us, that which can keep us on course and away from the rocks in the sea of life.

When the orangutans are shrieking, it's especially difficult to find that quiet inner self. One of my tried and tested tricks on those days is to keep it simple. I close my eyes and listen. That's it. Listen to the hum of the refrigerator, the creaks and groans of our home as it expands and contracts in the changing temperatures. A dog barking, crows cawing, Willy Wagtails singing, Garfield the Wonder Cat who can mend a broken heart stretching and catching his claws in the fabric of the couch, a vehicle driving past the house or the sound of my breath moving through my nostrils. It's then time to move on to what my body can feel. The cool air on bare skin, the warmth of my clothing, the spread of my thighs and butt on the floor or chair, the snug fit of elastic on underwear. There's also the feeling of one part of my body touching another, the warmth of the hair on my head, the twinge in my right hip, the heavy sadness in my heart or perhaps the effervescent joy bubbling up in me. It's about connecting with yourself in any given moment and acknowledging what is. Not asking for anything, not wanting to change anything. Simply opening up to a full awareness of this moment. Try it. I guarantee you'll open your eyes feeling calmer, more centred and somehow different.

I'm not a great believer in asking for things. I know some people believe that prayer or meditation will deliver what you want. If it doesn't, it wasn't in God's plan. What I ask for is comfort and peace. I've found myself sobbing over the tragic loss of a young, precious life with no idea how to navigate this raw pain. I asked whatever or whoever was out there listening (at least I hoped it was listening) to "please bless me with comfort and peace."

Sure enough, a measure of comfort and peace was mine in that moment and many, many more moments like it throughout my life. A connection with the Divine, or whatever you know it as, can sustain and support us. It can give us strength when we are weak.

All it asks of us is that we remember that it's out there, and make some time to tune in now and again. Like our mums, all it really wants is for us to call on it once in a while to say thanks for being there.

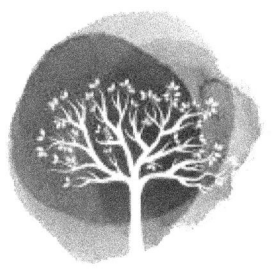

Chapter 15

Pen your thoughts
We write to taste life twice
~ Anais Nin

Like a stealthy pirate, the feeling can sneak up on you. One day, you realise that there's nothing left in you – you're hollow. Empty. Aching. What a rotten day. But actually, it is, in fact, a great day. Because now you know, now you've acknowledged just how lousy you feel. And having acknowledged it, you can do something about it. Move forward. Honour yourself. Heal. This day is, in fact, cause for great celebration. You just don't know it yet.

I suspect that one way or another, we've all been in that place. The one we can't get out of fast enough, but seem to be stuck in for what feels like a long, long, time…

One of the ways I have clawed my way back to the beauty of the world has been writing in a journal. Re-reading bits and pieces makes me realise how much raw beauty was right there in front of me, how much delight and joy I can get today from revisiting the perfectly ordinary moments of my days and relishing the wonder and unique beauty that lies in tiny, seemingly insignificant things. I once learned a technique to bind a book which can be used as a journal. It's such a lovely thing that I decided to use it only to record beauty, joy and all the loveliness the world showed me. I wasn't about to sully this special thing with ugly, miserable thoughts and ideas!

There is something about the weight and feel of it in my hands that gives me comfort. It's beauty is in its intention – the careful and thoughtful gathering and selecting of papers, the contemplative nature of stitching it all together is somehow soothing and calming. I've since made a number of these as gifts, and every time, they are received with delight. You begin by cutting heavy card to size for the covers and choose a selection of papers that will please you – different colours, textures and weights, some with rough, uneven edges, some slick and sharp. Choosing the papers is possibly my favourite part – the feel of tissue and fine papers, the colour of bright and lively ones, the solid, reliable strength of heavier pages. The glow and buzz of the bundle begins as the collection comes together and you imagine how it will look once completed and how it might feel in your hands. Then the stitching begins. Slow, careful, firm but gentle – a delicate balance of tight enough to make the book strong but gentle enough not to tear through the entire bundle of papers which is such a bummer if you happen to have that happen! There is such sweet satisfaction as the bundle of loose folded sheets slowly becomes a solid journal. Each new 'signature' added builds the sense of accomplishment and delight. Seemingly suddenly, it's complete! You hold in your hands a thing that fills you with satisfaction, with a great sensate pleasure, and for a moment, the world is perfect.

I guess that's what I'm trying to say here, for us to seek out the little ways that we can, even for just a brief moment, pronounce our world as 'perfect'. Digging back though my journals, I've found this collection of moments. Reading them transports me back to those moments with such clarity and vivid detail, it's as if I'm reliving them over again:

It's eight weeks until my first-born child Fraser is getting married! I remember the day he was born so vividly. There he was with his enormous eyes watching me so intently from the crib across from me and sucking his thumb! He 'lost' that thumb after the first hours of his life and it took him a couple of weeks to find it again. What a miracle a child is and continues to be. It seems moments ago that he was that tiny baby, which was followed by the small child with sturdy limbs and a questioning mind; the little boy nervously starting school; the teenager confidently leaving home for boarding school. And before I knew it, here was a young man hopping on a plane bound for the other side of the world. I'll soon watch him marry a wonderful woman; a girl who has carved her own special place in my heart.

Is there a mother alive who doesn't know the bittersweet beauty of a child growing up, becoming an adult, taking the world in their stride? I doubt it. I'm constantly fascinated at how proud and happy and wistful I can be all at once!

It's a pretty big deal to watch your child become a husband - a wonderful, heartwarming, happy, beautiful, big deal.

His expression as she made her way to him made my heart happy. 'Cos his heart looked happy - know what I mean?

So many ordinary moments, caught on the page, remind me that even the mundane, ordinary days hold beauty if we just take a moment to stop and look:

It feels like a perfect morning. There's a gentle breeze and it's clear and bright. The day holds such promise. It's quiet, peaceful. Just the sound of so many birds and my own breath. Every so often the clip of a dog's toenails on the concrete outside and the odd pant as one of our four-legged friends trots by, going about the important business of being a dog!

What's beautiful? The smell of lavender on the cleaning cloth, as the glowing timber surfaces are revealed from under the dust and clutter and the soothing scent lingers in the room. There's the squeak of the cleaning cloth on sparkling mirrors and glass, the feeling of clean feet on clean cork tiles and the slight tapping sound when you walk across it. There's the beauty of silence when the vacuum cleaner is finally turned off and the physical weariness after a day of bending, stretching, carrying and lifting. It's a tired body, but a satisfied one that feels the pleasure of the work, knowing a sound sleep awaits...

Re-reading that passage almost made me want to stop writing to go and clean the house! Almost...

I'm enjoying the cool change, pulling the doona up around my chin in bed. Snuggling in is so much nicer than laying sprawled out trying not to let any one part of your body touch another in an attempt to find some kind of relief from the relentless heat and humidity! The warmth of the sun on my face is like a caress instead of a blast furnace! The lorikeets have come to feed on the flowers of the Swamp Bloodwood offering noisy, raucous splashes of colour and energy that you can't help but feel a little lighter after hearing and seeing them.

This morning, I got a call for an 'all-terrain puppy rescue'! Heading to the sand ridge on the four-wheeler was brisk! Not sure why I didn't put a coat on... The cold morning air on the chest and face is bracing, to say the least! But, the clear, cloudless sky and freshness of the morning were beautiful. Our dog Darla perched up in front of me, licking my face! There we were riding along, enjoying the clarity of the light, with two tiny red birds darting in and out of the long grass below.

I am thankful for clean clothes, for funny dogs, for lavender oil, for the rose smell in my jumper when I pulled it on this morning, for moonlit nights and their liquid beauty. For never having to be hungry. For pens and paper and silence and breeze rustling the leaves in the trees. For photographs – memories every one, of ordinary days, happy times, moments, caught to be relived and remembered forever. I am thankful for sunshine, my garden that grows and flourishes in spite of me and sometimes dies, as things must. I am also grateful for ordinary moments – tea and toast for breakfast in my jim jams, the rhythms of unpacking the dishwasher, hanging out washing, creating a meal. Tiny golden moments – a laugh shared between the boys, good-natured teasing, a small kindness.

Alan feeding the chooks and Keelan taking out the rubbish. They are little, routine things that magically make up a day, and then another, then another...adding up to a full life.

I look forward to the smiles and beautiful eyes of my sons, the beauty of the natural world around me, the vision of Alan coming toward me with mischief in his eyes. I enjoy being able to read and write, the ability to look at art and photography and colours and patterns and textures and hearing the voices of those I love. I look forward to hearing them share their dreams, ideas, excitement, sadness and delight. To listen lovingly to others and feel valued for that. The smell of cakes cooking, freshly-mown grass, White Linen perfume, white flowers, rain, lavender, clean sheets, old books, lamb shanks cooking, garlic and onion frying. The smell of horses, the particular scent of massage oil. The taste of chocolate, curry, lemon - combinations of flavour that delight....caramel, malt, cinnamon, mango. To feel a hug, a pat on the back, a gentle touch. Feeling the comfort of clothes, bed linen, the firm support of the floor beneath, the caress of fresh air on bare skin; the warm, soothing flow of water in a shower.

I feel myself relax, my breath slow down and deepen, my shoulders lower, my pulse steady...all that happens in my body simply when I sit with a journal in my lap.

An early start gave me the chance to sit with my cup of tea and watch the clouds drift lazily across a pre-sunrise sky. A beautiful moment – interrupted by a visit from a brown snake! It scared the crap out of me and I jumped and spilled tea in my lap!
My half hour walk in complete peace is restorative to my soul… to see the sun poking up over the horizon, the dogs bounding in and out of the long grass, flushing out quail and other birds and chasing ducks off the dam, making me laugh out loud. The feeling of my blood pumping all around my body, my breath filling my lungs with fresh, crisp, early morning air. The 'bubbly' feeling in my legs after I've walked for a while and the strength I feel building in myself as I stride along, head up, breathing in life and possibility. I love the beauty of each fresh, new day as it dawns, each sky a little different, each walk offering up news sights, sounds, and smells. There's the eight pelicans that flew overhead, skidding to rest on Bell Lagoon dam. Beauty, wonder and drama are revealed on every journey!
Choc-chip biscuits that turned out perfectly (in my mind at least!) with their delicious combination of salty crunch, sweet softness and chocolate goo. Scented candles, Earl Grey tea, hot showers, soft sheets, the feel of silk, beautiful colours, old buttons, hot chocolate, candlelit bath soaks, the glow and shine of coloured glass, a visit to the hairdresser, a glass of wine while watching the day fade away. Then there's rainy days, beautiful days, delicious soup, hugs, friends, laughter, sharing warmth and the sensation of warm water on a cold day…

Capturing those moments is a gift to my future self. They serve as a reminder that the smallest things hold beauty and sweetness; that when all is said and done, I am lucky beyond measure.

I have other journals, too. They are cheap, spiral-bound notebooks. My favourite one proclaims on the front cover "I'm not weird. I'm a limited edition". These are the pages into which I pour my frustration, irritation, hurt and anger. I don't bother to re-read these. I appreciate the job they do as a rubbish tip for the less comforting contents of my mind, and the release that comes with tearing out the pages and burning them is immense, because I am letting go of whatever is making me unhappy.

I know we aren't all writers. For some of us, writing feels like a chore, a task to be completed. One of the things I love about my journals is that they are for my eyes only (and yours, now that the contents are tipped out here!) I don't need to write neatly - or even legibly! I love having the freedom of tripping over words, misspelling them, sometimes even only getting half a word written at a time, as my mind sails ahead and my hand races to keep up. I can confess that spelling and grammatical errors are one of my pet peeves. If I discover a spelling mistake in a blog post, I am quick to correct it. If I make an error in a comment online somewhere and am unable to correct it, I can need counselling! (OK, not quite...but it troubles me a lot!)

But in my journal, I have freedom. There is no censoring, no re-reading to polish the words and smooth them out, just the pleasure of feeling me hear myself, of making sense of the jumble of thoughts, feelings and ideas that sometimes congest my mind.
In the interests of 'keeping it real', I should tell with you that those excerpts I've shared here are my favourites, the pieces of writing that I love to re-read. There is a great deal more writing that is tedious, ordinary, uninteresting and often illegible! Our journal writing isn't intended to be a polished breathtaking thing of beauty. The purpose of it is to be a catch-all for our thoughts. It captures our trials, our triumphs, our heartbreaks and our happiness. The point and purpose of journal-keeping is not to write. It is to help our heads and hearts process our human experience and create a space for us to rest, be present and pay attention.

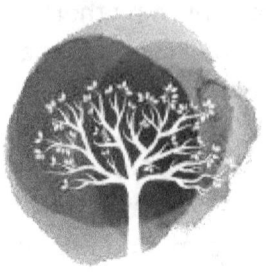

Chapter 16

Be who you want to be

My happiness grows in direct proportion to my acceptance and in inverse proportion to my expectations.~ Michael J Fox

Expectations. Acceptance. I believe these two are opposite sides of the same coin. I feel lucky to have arrived in this world as a human who is relatively accepting. My first instinct is to look for the best in people, and - with the odd rare exception - I can usually find something to love, or at the very least like or admire, in everyone I come across. Which makes accepting them as they are, for who they are pretty easy.

I suspect that sometimes, I'm seen by some as too easy; too forgiving, unreasonably kind and generous. There have been times I've wondered if perhaps that is true - am I, in fact, so easy on others that I let them walk all over me? In some instances, that may be true. But do you know what I continually come back to? The knowledge - deep in my bones - that my life is easier, sweeter and freer when I can let others be. Let them be exactly who they are. Accept their personalities, their stories and their quirks and foibles. Accept their behaviour in as much as it doesn't harm me or anyone else (in which case, I need to take responsibility for dealing with that in a manner that respects me and them).

Our community was fortunate to be visited by author and CEO of the Quest For Life Foundation, Petrea King in the aftermath of the 2011 floods. Petrea's visit was to offer some ideas and insight into how to build resilience into ourselves and, as an extension of ourselves, our families and community. She had so much to offer, and the days I spent listening to her share stories and ideas were to be tremendously helpful to me. Petrea has a few formulas into which we can insert words to help us have challenging conversations - with ourselves and with others. One that I have held close and remembered well helps us to step outside of another's difficult, frustrating or challenging behaviour and get some perspective and peace. We will always encounter other people who - for whatever reason - rub us the wrong way, press our buttons and possibly make us a bit nuts. If you don't have at least one of these people in your orbit somewhere, go find one! They offer endless opportunities for you to grow.

Imagine this...

Your crazy-making-person (the one whose behaviour can take your perfectly good mood and leave you wanting to scream in frustration) is becoming unbearable. For the purpose of this conversation, let's name her Agnes. I don't know anyone named Agnes, so if this is your name, please forgive me, I'm sure you're wonderful! Please feel free to insert the name of your own crazy-making person here. Agnes is being demanding, difficult and saying and doing things that are pressing your buttons and making you light up like a poker machine. Petrea suggests you quietly, calmly, tell yourself this:

"Ah, look. There's Agnes, doing Agnes. Being the person she is and doing all she can. No one does Agnes better than Agnes does...If I want Agnes to be any different from Agnes, I am going to suffer."

Of course I am going to suffer - because Agnes can't do anything BUT be Agnes. When we realise this and fully understand that

Agnes is doing the best she can, doing the only thing she knows that will get her needs met (even if it's completely inappropriate and unreasonable), we can accept that this is the way she is. We can take a little step back and secure our boundaries. Because it's wonderful to let Agnes be, but it's not okay for her 'being' to damage ours. Acceptance is peace. Acceptance is NOT buying into Agnes's drama. It's NOT letting her say and do whatever she wants, without repercussion. Acceptance is acknowledging that there are things beyond our control, and who Agnes is as a person is one of those things.

Life doesn't always go the way we plan. Our expectations are sometimes dashed on the rocks of reality. God knows, I've made at least a million plans that have not seen the light of day. Perhaps being a farmer's wife teaches you hard and fast that what you expect and what eventually happens are seldom the same thing. My mum has observed that I may make Plan A, but what I eventually execute will probably look more like Plan F7. Sometimes, Plan F7 is way cooler than Plan A. Often Plan F7 is a disappointing suck-fest! The wheat harvest that was looking like it would yield two tonne to the acre and easily pay the interest bill to the bank (with a little left over) is rained on, sprouts on the plant before it can be harvested, and we're lucky beyond measure to find a sale for it at all. Or, I'm cold, tired, filthy and desperate for a hot shower, and the pressure pump has burnt out, so tonight's ablutions will take place in the hand basin with whatever water was in the kettle, and I won't be brushing my teeth, or flushing the toilet until the pressure pump is replaced. (For the uninitiated, when you live without town water, you rely on a pressure pump to fill your pipes. No pressure pump, no water. The end.) Or, I expect 60 people to arrive for a special birthday celebration, a crazy storm blows in, dumps six inches of rain, and the road is cut. At least we now have enough steak to feed ourselves for a month. Or, the same kind of storm blows in, only this time the car is packed and ready for a much-anticipated and needed weekend away. I'm left with no option but to unpack the car, cancel the booking and choose how to feel about this turn of events. I think you get the idea. We make plans, we have expectations, life happens and the goal posts move.

Sometimes those expectations are so horribly dashed that it's a major life-changing event. Other times, it means you need to wash the sheets as soon as the pressure pump is fixed. Either way, our capacity to accept the cards we have been dealt will determine how much peace and happiness we can find on the journey. How easily we are able to adjust (or completely abandon) our expectations, will determine our ability to find some grace.

Accepting things the way they are makes life easier.

Let me say that again - accepting things as they are makes life easier. It doesn't mean we settle. It doesn't mean we stop working toward things being better. It doesn't mean we give up on our dreams and longings. Quite the opposite. Accepting things as they are right now frees up our energy. Then we can do what we need to do to make things the way we want them to be rather than clinging on to unmet expectations for dear life and obsessing over how things aren't the way we believe they 'should' be.

This brings me, perhaps a little uncomfortably, to self-acceptance. If I'm espousing acceptance as a path to peace, freedom and ease, I have to acknowledge and admit that accepting myself exactly for who I am is every bit as important as accepting others; every bit as significant as accepting circumstances.

This is interesting. Since I began writing this part about self-acceptance (all 50 words of it), I have needed a glass of water, clicked across to my email, read six, answered two and read two resumes and a cover letter from a couple wanting to work on our farm. Seems I will do ANYTHING to avoid thinking about accepting myself. Because, the truth of the matter is that I have a lot of room for growth in that department. Now, when things are humming along okay, and my work in the office is under control and up to date and the house and yard are more or less tidy and clean, and my family all seem happy, and I'm getting into my studio most days, and my clothes fit well and my hair is behaving, I would clearly and surely tell you I accept myself the way I am. That perfect alignment of circumstances happens for roughly two days every three years! The remainder of the time, I am guilty of holding myself ransom to my own outrageous expectations. "I'll give you my total acceptance just as soon as you are perfect." It's that or something equally ridiculous and impossible.

I could sit here for the next three days and work hard on blaming all kinds of people and circumstances and situations and experiences for my struggle with self-acceptance. Or, I can once again notice it, apologise to myself and choose to pay attention. Choose to stop expecting things from myself that I would expect from no other mortal. As writer Elizabeth Gilbert suggests, choose instead to embrace the glorious mess. How much easier and simpler and kinder will that be? This is a shift I have been working on for a while but I forget. I slip into old habits, re-run old scripts. Then I remember and start over.

It would be easier - and feel ever so much less vulnerable - to pretend that a great measure of self-acceptance is mine than to admit to that particular resource being scarce. But, I know I'm not alone. I am acutely aware that others punish themselves with this same withholding of self- acceptance, and I suspect that - to some extent at least - we are all pretending. All straining to appear as though we are confident, strong and sure of ourselves; when in fact, we are often uncertain, and wishing we were somehow better.

What I am certain of is that the more fully able I am to accept what life throws at me, then the happier, calmer and freer I find myself. It follows then, that - imperfections and all - the more fully I can accept myself, the deeper and sweeter my happiness, calm and freedom will feel.

Work cited: Petrea King, Your Life Matters, Random House, Sydney, 2004

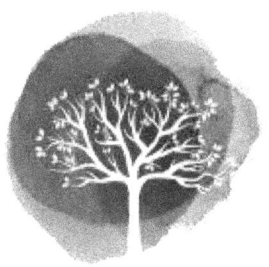

Chapter 17

Riding the boundary

Daring to set boundaries is about having the courage to love ourselves, even when we risk disappointing others. ~Brene Brown

They say good fences make good neighbours. As an owner of cows and other assorted animals, I know this to be true. Keeping your livestock where it belongs and protecting your boundaries from roaming intruders is an important responsibility. It helps keep your own stock safe from disease, keeps roaming animals from chewing down the feed your own stock need, and it keeps the general public safe. After all, hitting a cow with your Corolla is never going to end well.

When your boundaries are in bad repair, or worse still, they have fallen down or are non-existent, it isn't clear to stock where they can and cannot roam. This ultimately creates friction, extra work and aggravation for those whose boundaries are left unattended. For someone who has such a deep understanding and appreciation of the value and critical importance of property boundaries, I realise the irony in my struggle to set personal boundaries. This is because the same impacts can apply to our personal boundaries as to our property boundaries. Healthy personal boundaries can keep us well and ensure we remain well-nourished. The safety of the general public is also better ensured when we honour our own need for space and when we protect our time and energy from roaming intruders.

It was in the middle of my life-altering-Kryptonite-impact-episode that my need to draw a few lines in the sand and proclaim "This far and NO further!" became unavoidably apparent. I was part way through a kinesiology treatment when the kinesiologist Joe said to me "You have a hard time setting boundaries, don't you?" Kinesiology is something which I highly recommend as the kinesiologist works with your electromagnetic fields and balances your energy. They can 'shift' stuff you didn't even know was clogging up your energy flow. I always walk out of a kinesiology session feeling like a million bucks. On this occasion, tears stung my eyes, and while my brain was saying "No, no!" my soul was clearly saying "Finally... Yes. Thank you."

I've had a hard time with boundaries because I want to make everybody happy. I want to give everyone everything they want. I want everything to be right. (Read "I expect myself to attain perfection All. The. Fucking. Time.").

But somewhere along the road, my brain got wired (or possibly wired itself - who knows?) to believe that taking care of everyone else would ensure that I would remain loved. I've got to tell you - it's taken years of digging and poking around in the dark recesses of my mind to come to this realisation. It almost sounds too simple there, just like that. Of course, that lies at the bottom of layers and layers of other thought patterns, which are equally limiting and damaging. But, I think this is at the very core.

When you finally realise that you need to set some boundaries and defend them, it can feel like you're setting yourself up for a re-enactment of the Gallipoli landing. After all, 30 years of agreeably nodding and doing the best I could to accommodate requests for all kind of things, ranging from "Jump up and bring me a beer." to "You'll organise a photography exhibition, won't you?" Other examples include: "Come and rub my neck" and "My photos aren't on this computer anywhere! See if you can find them." Of course they were, and I did, many times). Over the years, I've had the people in my life, ranging from the closest family members through to acquaintance, comfortable in the knowledge that I would be the one to ask for what they wanted and knowing they would get it.

Beginning to set some boundaries was terrifying. The idea of saying "I can't", "Maybe later" or, most shocking of all, "I don't want to", had me bracing for some kind of nuclear fallout. But guess what? It wasn't that bad. I was gritting my teeth and holding my breath and expecting tantrums and resistance for which I wasn't entirely sure I could maintain my wall of defence. Instead, what I mostly found was proof of the theory that if you respect yourself, others will also respect you. Instead of Gallipoli, I mostly got Lake Louise.

I found that when I can say what I need, or what I am able to offer, and what is off the table, people around me are generally pretty fine with it. I didn't suddenly stop doing anything for anyone at all. After all, the giving and helping of others is my superpower. What I found was that when I started to check my boundary fences often, I was able to strain up the wires in a couple of places that had been a constant source of worry, with stray cows wandering in and chewing down my nourishment. Once that was done, I discovered I seemed to have more to give, rather than less, and was much happier giving it.

It continues to require day by day diligence to check those fences; and it's certainly easier to slip into old habits sometimes. But it's the old story that what has been seen cannot be unseen. I know what I need to do. I know how to do it.

I simply need to choose to keep riding those boundaries and checking those fences. My choice. My responsibility. My bloody fence.

As I ponder this new routine, I find myself remembering a little story about a different boundary infraction:

I've been working on my bookwork for a couple of solid hours and I'm quite absorbed in getting the pile of paper in front of me processed and loaded into the computer. I've been vaguely aware of an odd noise outside. A frog, sounding as though the wicked witch of the west has him strung up on a rack is emitting a slow, steady croak that just doesn't sound quite right. As I work, he croaks and squeaks away. This processing needs to be finished so I can lodge the Business Activity Statement (BAS) which is due tomorrow. So I keep going, occasionally wondering what the frog's problem is as I flip to a new page. Finally, I can stand it no longer. As I throw the office door open, there's an odd rustling sound by my right ear. Turning, I'm thrown into a cold panic as there is a very big snake right beside my ear, wending his way up the brick wall headed for that tiny gap between the top of the brickwork and the underside of the roof.

He can't fit in there, I assure myself, as I run through the options available to me most of which involve me getting much closer to this slimy reptile than I would like. My God, he's huge! Keelan is the only one within a range to be helpful, so a quick call gets him headed my way. But Hagrid has other ideas. Okay, so I named the snake. I've seen this sucker once a summer for three years now and every year he gets a little bigger. He's big, he's ugly and is terrifying in appearance. I suspect he wouldn't harm anyone, but I'm far from certain. Doesn't that sound just like Harry Potter's friend Hagrid? So, Mr Snake, from this moment on, thou shalt be known as Hagrid. Hagrid may be described by some as beautiful. (I am not including myself among them) He is at least 6 feet long, slender, olive green, with a pattern of vivid blue specks along his side. If he didn't scare the crap out of me so much, I could be quite captivated by his markings.

By the time Keelan arrives, Hagrid is 12 inches into the roof, his substantial body twisting and writhing to squeeze into the tiny hole which I believe he has used to access our roof many times before. Although today, he has a bellyful of frog which shows as a big bulge in his middle. Surely, he can't get in there with that big lump in his guts? Wrong. Again. By some astonishing feat of natural versatility, Hagrid manoeuvres himself and squeezes his round two and a half inch body into a one and three quarter inch hole, where the corrugated iron of the roof sits up off the brickwork. Shit. Hagrid is in my roof. And, judging by the deft way he gained access, I'm guessing he's done it a time or two before today.

Perhaps Hagrid's residence up there keeps us from having mouse infestations. We don't see too many mice, but I often hear an odd rustling noise in the ceiling and can't help but look up and pray there are no weak spots there. If Hagrid should fall through the ceiling into my lap – or, God forbid, into our bed as we sleep – I feel certain my heart would not withstand the shock. Did I mention he is BIG?

I consider my home, and it's walls, to be my safest refuge in the world. Those walls are definite, indisputable boundaries. When I got to thinking about Hagrid, and his quiet, slithery infiltration of those boundaries, it occurs to me that our personal boundaries can be compromised in similar ways. We can have the strongest walls in the world but if they have one tiny weak point - one vulnerable spot - our worst nightmare can slide right on in, often without us even knowing. While we are busy taking our safety and security for granted, the odd noises we hear when our house is quiet can unsettle us. Terror and fear may have already moved right in and all we have is a vague sense of unease.

I want very much at this point to deliver some sage wisdom and lightness. There's a snake in my ceiling, but I'm talking about how important it is to protect our boundaries so we aren't infiltrated by things that can harm us. Or might harm us. Or maybe, might in fact help us? So is that boundary breakdown so terrible after all? Yes.

Yes, it is. Because I thought I didn't have the choice. I thought there was no opportunity for me to evaluate and choose whether it might be beneficial to me. Hagrid got into the roof, whether I said it was okay or not. When I saw him coming, I was paralyzed with fear and stood, slack-jawed and incredulous. I watched him gain access without putting up any kind of fight.

Setting boundaries can be easy, especially with people who love, value and respect us. I'm getting better at it all the time; but protecting my boundaries from people and situations that have no regard or respect for our need for those boundaries, can call on us to face down our fear, dig very deep, put up a fight, and risk possible harm. Otherwise, we stand by, helpless to defend ourselves and spend weeks (or months, or even years), tiptoeing around afraid of what might fall into our laps, while the boundary crosser lurks in our shadows (or ceilings, as the case may be).

Thanks Hagrid, it turns out your visit that day just taught me something important. Next time though, would you kindly take yourself up a hollow log like the rest of the reptilian population?

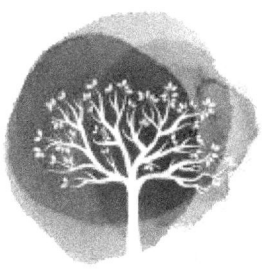

Chapter 18

You've got a radio on board
Be strong enough to stand alone, smart enough to know when you need help, and brave enough to ask for it.~ Ziad K. Abdelnour

Regardless of how proficient we become at sailing, how experienced we might be at navigating and steering, even the saltiest old sailors sometimes get into difficulties that require them to call for help. Our self-propelled boats come fitted with communication devices which allow us to radio for assistance so you should use it. If you found yourself on the ocean with swells rising, your boat taking on water and a hole in the hull, the first thing you'd do would be to pick up that handset and radio the coastguard.

I've lost count of the number of times my mind has resembled this impending maritime disaster. Did I radio for help? Oh hell no. In spite of being fortunate enough to have endless resources available to me in the way of friends, family, and wellbeing services, I told myself others are worse off than I am (truth be known, they were), and I'll get through this. Struggle, grope, grasp, cry, despair, beat myself up and do it all again tomorrow. And the next day, and the day after, and the day after that.

God only knows where I developed the notion but somehow I seemed to believe that I should be able to manage all on my own...

everything, all the time. (You know - like the old Eagles song). To ask for help somehow confirmed that I was incapable, useless and unreliable. The irony is that when others need help, I'm among the first to listen, support and reassure them that they're going to be okay, and help them find the help they need.

I'll never forget the day I finally dissolved into tears in the lap of my precious friend Diana, when I finally admitted that I wasn't managing the ongoing feelings of anxiety that seemed to have taken up residence under my skin. I felt exposed, vulnerable and utterly terrified. Interestingly, when I recently spoke with Diana about it, she has only a vague memory of that day. Admitting my fragility and asking for support felt so enormous and so life-threatening that the moment is burned in my memory with acute detail. For Di, it was just another day to be a kind friend. The moment for her was without any judgement that I was a failure or weak, or any of the other nonsense I was telling myself. My discomfort in sharing my feelings with her was nothing compared to the magnitude of feelings swimming through me as I sat in Dr Bruce's room, confessing what seemed to me to be my gross inadequacies. Diana made me promise I would go and see him, for which I am eternally thankful. I will never forget the sweet relief and reassurance when he told me the tomato stand story. YES! I'd given away all my tomatoes, and forgotten that I somehow needed to replenish the source.

I hated taking those bloody anti-depressants that were prescribed. But just as Dr Bruce promised, it wasn't long before the old me started to wake up once again. I read a lot, researched more, and set about building myself a set of resources that would support me, which have ultimately become the stars by which I navigate. I wanted those tablets out of my life, as soon as possible. Dr Bruce said six months. So that's how long I took them for and not a day longer. Let me tell you something. Stopping those Zoloft tablets cold turkey wasn't the smartest thing I've ever done! By the time I realised that the weird stuff going on in my body was basically

withdrawals, I was too far gone to go back. It was an unpleasant month or two with the sensation of a bunch of alien creatures having moved in under my skin, but by then I'd developed a bunch of other strategies to get through it. Once again though, I now realise that I didn't ask for help. I just did it. I could have made it much easier for myself (and undoubtedly on my family) if I had sought assistance to bring that to an end but I didn't.
I know I'm not alone in my reluctance to ask for help. Or, perhaps it's more accurately a reluctance to even admit to myself that I might need help. I remind myself of a recalcitrant two year old, snatching away her shoes, frowning and pouting "I do it myself!"

It wasn't until I had begun writing this book, and came up with the analogy of sailing life's waters, that I realised how important our own radios are. When you are taking on water, you call the coastguard. It's much easier, cheaper and quicker to save you if you are in a viable vessel with full radio communication.
If you wait until the boat is as good as sunk, your rescue becomes more dangerous for everyone. Calling for help is a huge relief, it might be uncomfortable at first to admit you're struggling - after all, you believe you are the unsinkable Titanic (and we all know what happened to that!). But knowing that help is at hand immediately diffuses the tension and anxiety. The knowledge that you don't have to go it alone any longer is a sweet relief. That old adage really does hold true - a problem shared is a problem halved. Going off that metric, a problem shared a few times, with a few safe and trusted friends, becomes exponentially reduced. And the particular suffering you want to share the least? That's the one you need to share the most.

Chapter 19

The choice is yours
I am not what happened to me, I am what I choose to become.
~CG Jung

"We are all responsible for our own happiness."
"No one else can make us happy. We have to choose that and work on that for ourselves."

The dissatisfied and unhappy woman I'm talking with doesn't take this idea well. For her, it's easier if it's someone else fault. When the problem is 'out there', we can feel sorry for ourselves. We don't need to take responsibility for our own happiness because it's out of our control.

The notion that we cannot be happy because someone else isn't the way we want them to be only gives away our power. We think that they mustn't love us because they are being themselves instead of forcing themselves into our own peculiar version of a wonderful partner, friend or family member. The truth is that we will never change another person with the force of our will. What we can do - the only thing that we can do - is focus on what it is we appreciate about them. At the same time, we can be checking in with ourselves to discover the little things which we hunger for to feed our happiness. Then we can make sure we give ourselves those things. We choose. We choose to see the positives. We choose what we focus on. We choose how we are going to respond to any given situation. We choose to be in charge of our own joy and happiness.

I've talked about making choices a number of times in this book. It seems to me that just about everything we encounter on this journey comes down to a choice between swabbing the decks of our dreamboat and checking our course regularly or laying in the sun expecting everything to take care of itself. Or perhaps we are peering out across the water, muttering under our breath about the hurricanes and pirates and blaming them for all of our challenges and setbacks.

I've realised that this journey can be simple and delightful if I stay aware and keep choosing to check my compass and use the instruments with which my dreamboat came equipped. But, if I choose only to look overboard, out to the horizon, and give control of my destiny to the pirates and hurricanes, I'm almost certain to be miserable.

We choose. All the time, every moment of our lives, we are making choices. What to cook for dinner, when to drink a glass of water. Whether to buy the shoes. Which road to take to work. How to use our time. An infinitesimal number of choices happen before we've even eaten breakfast on any given day without us even realising it. Most of the choices we make are so small and habitual we aren't even aware we make them. Routine takes over and instead of choosing, we do what we've always done.

Choosing to choose isn't easy. Sometimes it's bloody hard work. Especially when the choices we have available to us aren't the ones we want. We can sit back and let circumstances roll across us and tell ourselves we couldn't change them. Or, we can notice our options, acknowledge we don't like any of them, and choose one anyway. That choice has power. That choice says to the Universe or whomever you subscribe to: "I am ready to take responsibility for my life. I want this to be different, but for now, I'm choosing this option." Because life doesn't always deliver the option we want when we want it. But it always delivers us a choice.

Sometimes, the only choice available to us is our attitude. Life has given me a number of opportunities to learn this - crashing to the ground from a galloping horse being in poll position:

Keelan and I are yarding weaner cattle. Foolishly I have chosen to jump on a horse I've never ridden before, simply because he was saddled and I was too lazy to take the few minutes needed to catch and saddle my usual steed.

I have fallen off and hurt myself badly. A broken scapula, snapped in half with the detached part smashing into the ribs beneath and breaking a few of them. This accident ranks among the highest impacting events in of my life, in more ways than one! Keelan and I almost had those weaners yarded, when Syd (thereafter referred to as the big brown bastard) got a bee up his butt and went berserk. I can't have been meant to die. They say when you are about to check out, that everything slows down and your life flashes before your eyes (or is that just in the movies? I don't know anyone who's ever died that I can ask about that...) It happened so fast. I left the saddle heading to my right, head pointing north. I opened my eyes to find myself on my left side, head facing south – to this day I can't figure that one out. Now, I've given birth three times, and honestly, I would have preferred to deliver another baby than experience that pain. I could hear such terror in Keelan's voice as he called out to me, galloping across to where I lay on the ground and trying to make some sound to let him know that I was still alive. It must have been pretty scary to watch as he was sure my number was up.

The conversation went kind of like this:

"Are you okay?"

"No. Yes, but no"

"Well, you'll have to get up. You can't lie here. Those weaners might turn around and trample over the top of you, then you'd really be fucked."

Can't argue with the boy's common sense. I could possibly have taken issue with the bad language, but I was in too much pain to care. I kind of felt pretty much that way anyway.

He helped me to my feet as I really couldn't get up alone. But I kept telling the poor kid not to touch me. He walked me over to the remains of the hay bale the weaners had been feeding on, sat me up against it, and asked again if I was I alright? "Yes," I tell him. "Just go and call an ambulance." He turned around, swung a leg over his horse, and said:

"I'll just finish yarding these weaners first."
It's fair to say I was a little stunned. Then that wave of overwhelming pain washes over me. You know, when you hurt yourself and you know it hurts, and then after a few minutes something about it hits you like a Kenworth truck on a Northern Territory highway.

"Keelan!"

Horse spins around and races back to me.

"Are you right?"

"Yeah, but can you please call the ambulance before you yard up the weaners?"

"Oh – they won't take long; I'll do it as soon as I get them in the yard."

I watch the rump of his horse head off to finish this monumentally important task. Deep breath...okay, I run a mental check through my first aid training. I'm not in an altered conscious state, I'm not bleeding profusely anywhere, I'm not having too much difficulty breathing, I'm pretty certain I've broken something (or perhaps a number of somethings - the top right quarter of my torso and right arm felt like the Arkansas Axe Murderer had had a pretty good chop at them). My evaluation led me to believe my life wasn't in any danger and I wasn't about to die. So, I had to just get myself comfortable and wait. (A precious friend of mine later came to Keelan's defence, suggesting that he was scared and needed to do something. Yarding those weaners was something he knew he could do and get right.)

A couple of minutes later, the guy working for us appeared on a motorbike, and from my makeshift nest in the hay, I heard him call out to Keelan a few hundred yards away.
"Keelan, you want me to help you with these weaners?"
"No, I'm right Ben, but can you go and call Mum an ambulance? She's over there against that bale of hay."

Next thing I know, I am being showered in a hail of tiny pebbles, as Ben slides the motorbike in beside me sideways..."Are you okay?!"

"I'm okay, but I really need an ambulance- I've busted myself up pretty well."

Finally, someone was off to make that Triple Zero call.

Fast forward a week or so, past the hospital stay and out the other side of the drug-induced stupor I found myself in. During that time, I was completely incoherent but still feeling pain that rated eleven and a half on the 'out of ten' pain scale. There was no option to choose my way out of this particular situation. No use in my right arm, almost impossible to sleep, and in constant pain.

I feel the need to tell you here, that I have a pretty high pain threshold. Two of my babies were born without pain relief, and I can tolerate a fair bit of discomfort, as a rule. The only choice available to me was my attitude. Which, I have to confess was often not all that great. Eventually though, I realised that I could choose to be happy that I could manage to do a few things for myself rather than focus on all the things I couldn't. I could choose to be thankful that it was my shoulder that took the impact and not my head. I could choose to push hard and cause myself more pain, or stop trying to do everything I thought I should be trying to do and give my body the opportunity it needed to mend itself. It's true I had no choice about the injury. But there were still plenty of choices to make.

The choices we make largely determine the quality of our days. Of course, as the expression goes "shit happens". We all get our turn on the rocky, bumpy and difficult part of the road. None of us is immune to challenges, setbacks, losses, hurts and sorrows. But the choices we make about who we are and how we will meet these challenges determine whether we will find some moments of happiness and contentment along the way.

Remembering that I choose how to navigate life journeys, and what instruments and tools to use and when, is an enduring challenge. I still sometimes get caught on the merry-go-round of busyness and drama and forget that even that is a choice. In any given moment, I can choose to say "Not right now. Right now, I need to go for a walk." Or talk to my sister or lock myself in the studio for an hour or take a bath, or whatever it is I need in that moment to keep my boat sailing in the right direction.

When we say 'Yes' to one thing, we are saying 'No' to another. If we can remember that, and choose with purpose and grace, not only our days but also our minds and hearts will feel freer, easier and happier.

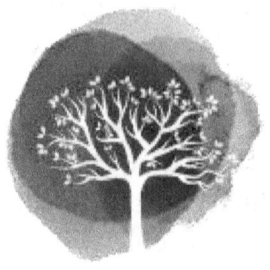

Chapter 20

The warm, safe glow of the lighthouse

A friend is someone who knows the song in your heart and can sing it back to you when you have forgotten the words.
~Unknown

Now, lighthouses aren't exactly on the list of standard accessories for our boats. But they are important. Really important. We all know lighthouses help prevent shipwrecks. They stand, strong and steadfast, shining a light into the dark and difficult passage of our journey.

As I've been contemplating our tools and maps, I've found myself returning to the thought that friends are a hugely important aspect of my journey, but they aren't exactly standard equipment on my boat. However, my boat would be less seaworthy without them. When one of my best friends (who just happens to be my sister) mentioned lighthouses in a conversation, it struck me. Our friends (and supportive family members who can sometimes be the best friends we ever have) are our lighthouses. And just as each lighthouse on the coast offers protection and illuminates different sectors of our journey, so too do each of our friends bless our lives with unique perspectives, complementing different parts of us. Lighthouses work with a small light source which is magnified by reflectors. Which is what are our friends are. They see our light - even when we feel it may have gone out altogether - and reflect it back to us so we might find our way home to ourselves once again. They can help us see the best version of ourselves, the person that they see and believe in, not the person we believe we are. I love to be a lighthouse for others. As I write this statement, it occurs to me that it may be the definition of my superpower. When I hop in my boat and take to the ocean, my sureness and steadiness gives way to the movement of the seas. But when I'm shining a light for someone else in the darkness is when I feel at my best.

While friends are far from being tools, instruments or maps for our journey, I know for sure that we need to include both them and the nurturing nature of our relationships with them on our list of resources. For I can be certain that when I have forgotten how to use my compass and my map has blown overboard, that my friends will keep shining their lights for me until I am safely in calm water once again.

What I'm trying to say is that we are responsible for our own happiness, choices, safety, health, and soul. In every area of our lives, the buck stops with us. BUT we need lighthouses. We need people who love us to reflect light on the dark places, and in turn, we need to be a lighthouse for others.

I am blessed beyond measure to have the best lighthouses on the planet. I hope with all my heart that my efforts as a lighthouse are as helpful, kind, supportive and loving as those I receive. It's funny that long ago I shared with some close friends the idea that I had read somewhere about us being 'from the same tree' (which could have been construed as a suggestion that we were monkeys, I guess!), Now here I am, writing my way through a wild ocean with a strong, safe tree standing tall on the horizon as my destination. I believe that tree on the distant shoreline is where our tribe shelters in the safe harbour. It is where our friends the lighthouse keepers, relieved of their posts, can come to rest. There we can share the tales of our collective adventures in safety, celebrating the safe delivery of our treasures to the shore. My lighthouses have indeed saved me from being shipwrecked on the rocks of my own doubts and insecurities, but nothing is sweeter than the moments spent together in the shelter of our tree.

Chapter 21

Coming home...to ourselves

We live on a blue planet that circles around a ball of fire next to a moon that moves the sea, and you don't believe in miracles?
~ Unknown

I'm now sailing very close to my destination. In fact, I think that magnificent old tree I set out in search of is coming into view on the horizon. This particular journey is almost over. When I set out, feeling strong and solid and unstoppable, I finally had my maps spread out on the bridge. This time, I knew where I was going. At least, I thought I did. What you hold in your hand isn't exactly the book I set out to write. It's more. I've learned many things in the writing, including small insights and big ah ha moments! They have come along to join me like dolphins riding a bow wave. My fondest hope is that you have found some of those as well. This began, as a rather long note to myself, exploring all the ways I had neglected to protect my treasure in the past and listing, for future reference, the multitude of options I have for protecting it from here on in.

In the course of the journey of writing this book, I have encountered every type of bad weather and a couple of pirates. Fear showed up on many occasions, determined to convince me of the mortal peril I would be placing myself in if I were to actually share these words with the world. Muriel, predictably, needed to be spoken to sternly on a number of occasions. I lost track of the number of times I suggested she get back to baking jam drops and leave me in peace. The awareness of their existence, and the ability to separate them from myself ever so slightly, made it possible to acknowledge the thoughts they were generating, while also recognising that those thoughts weren't all true stories.

The writing, on occasion, highlighted that I was not practicing what I was preaching. On countless occasions, I walked away from the work. I realised that I knew what I needed to do - I just needed to remember to do it!

I'm looking forward to resting under that tree, absorbing the wisdom I have gained along the way, and dreaming of the next adventure. I know I'll set out in my boat many more times. I also know that my compass and maps are at the ready, but they will need calibrating and updating. I know that all those tools and instruments are effective, but only if I choose to pick them up and use them.

It's time to embrace my Superpower. It is my deepest wish that you embrace yours too.

Grow she said...

Grow and stretch and expand and discover the amazing things you can do with this wondrous life you've been given

Open up, take deep breaths and inhale possibility

Let go of the thoughts and beliefs that hold you back

You were sent here to shine

So be free

Be bold

Be brave and find your wings and fly

Grow

So the world can have the very best of you

Everyone's waiting

Acknowledgement

How do I even begin to acknowledge all the love, support, encouragement, assistance and inspiration I have been the beneficiary of?

My grateful thanks goes to:

Kerrie Phipps, I think, gets first line credits. Kerrie's skill as a listener and coach helped me gather my vague, hazy thoughts so I could dig down to bedrock and excavate a whole slew of stuff that had been just beyond reach. Her encouragement and unwavering belief that I could do this surely was the embodiment of her motto - 'Cheering You On'. Cheer me on she did.

My family: Alan - for your unfaltering belief that I am capable of anything. Fraser, Fin and Keelan; you are my joy and my teachers. I have created a great many things in my life, but none I'm more proud of than the three of you. Leah, Caitlyn and Madi - our herd improvers! You three are my sweet reward for surviving a household full of males. Each of you has a beautiful heart, thank you for sharing it with me. Mum and Dad - for love and support and encouragement and all the good things parents are supposed to do - you nailed it. My sister Deb - the best lighthouse keeper this side of forever. Thanks for listening, offering wisdom, and believing in me. I've always felt that you were more Big Sister to me than the other way around. I am blessed beyond measure to have more lighthouses in Ralda Stainkey, Diana French, Kathy Poole, Meredith

Servin, Prue Davison, Kathy Sheehan and Julie Tyrer. Thank you for shining so brightly for me. Many of my life's happiest moments have been spent hanging out under our tree together.

The many students who have joined me in art workshops. I have learned so much more from all of you than I could ever hope to teach.

My editor, Natalie Holmes, who somehow managed to take my sometimes lumpy and clunky words, smooth them out, and send them back to me sounding silky and sage.

Caitlyn Hewitt, your enthusiasm for taking the 'portrait of the author' and turning an experience I was dreading into a bit of fun. Thank you for taking my awkward self and somehow capturing the 'real me' who had gone into hiding.

Dr Brene Brown, whose writing on courage, vulnerability and shame; and e-course have provided me with the places to find some big ah-ha! moments.

Your lesson on discovering our superpower and Kryptonite was powerful for me, and as you can see, has had far-reaching implications!

Elizabeth Gilbert, whose writing has gently guided me to redefine my relationship with fear, and generally inspired me to keep creating. Your Facebook page reminds me daily there is wonder and awesomeness in the world, and that social media can be a powerful force for good.

Lastly, my heartfelt thanks to every one of my family and friends who have helped keep me working toward finishing this book with their enthusiasm for the project and belief in my ability to execute it. Because of you, this book exists.

Resources

Books, blogs, websites and podcasts to accompany us on our journey:
Simple Abundance
by Sarah Ban Breathnach

The Gifts of Imperfection
I Thought It Was Just Me
Daring Greatly
Rising Strong
Ordinary Courage blog
by Brene Brown

The Desire Map
daniellelaporte.com
by Danielle la Porte

Big Magic
Big Magic Podcasts
Elizabeth Gilbert's Facebook page - seriously, this Facebook page is a life support system

The Artist's Way
Walking in this World
God is no laughing matter
By Julia Cameron

Your life matters
By Petrea King

Meditation apps

Stephanie Dowrick - Journal prompts etc

Connect with the author

Whether you're interested in finding out more about art journaling classes, having a look at Tracey's artwork or chatting about When Your Superpower Becomes Your Kryptonite, Tracey would love to hear from you.

Options for connecting include:

Website: traceyhewitt.com

Blog: traceyhewitt.blogspot.com

Email: tracey@traceyhewitt.com

Social Media:
    Instagram @traceyhewitt
    Facebook Tracey Hewitt Designs, Textile and Mixed Media Artist
    Twitter @Tracey_Hewit

Mailing Address:
PO Box 78
Theodore
Queensland
Australia 4719